how to make
and play the
DULCIMORE

Roy Acuff (left), the King of Country Music, accepts a dulcimore from Chet Hines for Opryland, U.S.A.

An
Early American Society
Book

how to
make
and play
the

DULCIMORE

Chet Hines

Stackpole Books

HOW TO MAKE AND PLAY THE DULCIMORE

Copyright © 1973 by
The Stackpole Company

Published by STACKPOLE BOOKS
Cameron and Kelker Streets
Harrisburg, Pa. 17105

Printed in the U.S.A.

Library of Congress Cataloging in Publication Data

Hines, Chet.
　　How to make and play the dulcimore

　　1. Dulcimer-Construction. I. Title.
ML1016.D8H5　　　787'.9　　　73-7509
ISBN 0-8117-0848-9

Contents

Foreword

In the summer of 1971 the Smoky Mountain Boys and I spent a week up in Montreal, Canada, playing at the U.S. Pavillion in a program called "Man and His World." We represented authentic country music. Bill Monroe had been there previously to represent Bluegrass music. There was a gentleman there working in a different part of the pavillion making the Appalachian dulcimore and demonstrating it, and I asked him to come down and be on my program. He played a number and the people were just delighted to see him working with us. While we were there he said, "Roy, I'd like to come down to the Grand Ole Opry sometime." I told him I was sure that Mr. Wendell would certainly be glad to have him. In October of that year he came down to Nashville and

Concert-size curly maple dulcimore made by Chet Hines and now at Opryland, U.S.A.

Another Hines-made concert model dulcimore.

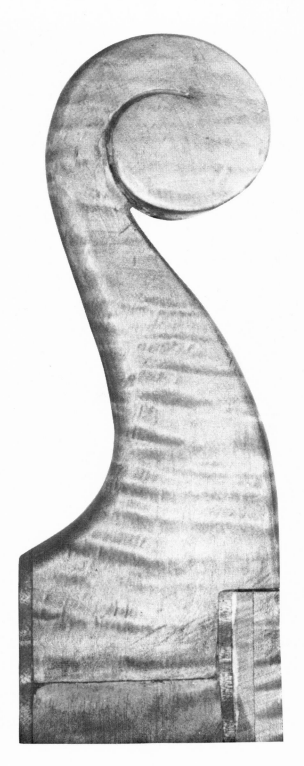

*Tuning head, curly maple
dulcimore.*

9

brought one of his very fine instruments and presented it to me for my museum, which is now a part of Opryland, U.S.A. The Appalachian dulcimore that he made for me is at Opryland among the many other fine instruments on display there. He brought another dulcimore with him that day, one that he had made of walnut, and played it on my show at the Grand Ole Opry.

The dulcimore is not a stranger at the Grand Ole Opry; we have had one or two players in past years and Chet does as good a job as any of them and the audience was delighted by his performance. We were proud to have him there to take part in our program.

To those of you who would like to make a dulcimore, or just learn to play it, I say good luck, work hard, and you could do no better than to have Chet Hines as a tutor.

Roy Acuff

Opryland U.S.A.
Nashville, Tennessee

Introduction

How shall we look at the American past?

For some, America a century ago was an Eden not yet lost. Life was hard but simple. Leisure was scarce and prized. Those whose lives depended on their own efforts were also masters of their own destinies. Today we look back in envious wonder at a time when (so it now seems) the world might leave the settler to die without aid, but it also left him to live without intrusion.

Some lonely few seek out our last remaining shreds of wilderness, and try to recapture that hard-earned freedom. The settlers and hill folk of a century ago stood on their own, but were not solitary. Their recreations and pleasures were communal, entwined with the community of work. The "mountain men" of today cannot hope to recapture the past; the best they can find is escape, which is not what 19th century America was about.

Some seek the simplicity and freedom of the past in its trappings and symbols: prairie dresses and fringed leather vests, candlelight and apple butter. Nostalgia for an unknown past has become the captivating fad of the day. Among young people who a little while ago were turning their backs on history, the nostalgic craze produces a muddled collage of Tiffany glass, pioneer dress, and the rhythms of the prohibition era, a shimmering surface of symbols that have largely lost their meanings.

Sophisticates look down and back at folk life and folk art, admiring its best products for their quaintness as much as for their beauty, cherishing the few nuggets of literary or artistic gold and sifting the dross back into the stream. Critical and selective collecting of folk art, polished and emended to fit refined standards of taste, has value in scholarship, and in the enrichment of contemporary life; but, like a museum, it is a contemporary institution, teaching us about the past by polishing and preserving its relics.

Another path is open to contemporary men and women who seek to recapture the past. We will be fed, transported, housed and perhaps enslaved by our machines. We will go on being enmeshed in the lives of others, men out of sight on the other side of the world whose lives and actions intrude upon our own. Without seeking to escape all this, one can choose some of the challenges of the past and try to master it. More and more people are turning to the crafts, the music, and the dance and games of 19th century America. To do so is to create in a corner of one's life the chance to do for oneself, instead of being done for (which so often means being done to). In that corner one can make a place in which the success or failure of what is attempted depends only on oneself. So it is that people are turning back to self-made music, to spinning and weaving, to pioneer cooking, natural dyeing, homemade balls for muzzle-loading rifles, handmade brooms and a hundred other challenges to the eye, the hand, and the patience of the craftsman. There is whimsy in it too; once you pick up the muzzle-loading gun, you are faced with the temptation of having the often store-bought coonskin cap. Sit before the spinning wheel and how can you not think of dressing in gingham and calico? If you boil dyes from roots and herbs, what more fitting vessel than an iron kettle over the fire?

Behind the whimsy is a warm reality—the chance to work with Nature, not against it, with the impulses of one's own heart, not against them, with the strength of one's own spirit, not in the yoke of a programmed social machine. This is not the search for a lost past, but the relearning of the lessons of the past. This is not the preservation of the relics of a lost life, but the reliving of one rewarding fragment of that life. This is not nostalgic longing for the good old days; modern handcrafts-men and folk musicians are not longing for the past, not saying "How sweet it was!" nor yet "How quaint!" They say simply: "This is how it was. It's still good."

* * *

I have a picture of Chet Hines in green fringed hunting shirt and three-cornered cap. He wears the costume with dignity and familiarity—but his mastery of the past would be as complete (but less at home) in white tie and tails. For more than a quarter of the century he has been making Appalachian dulcimores—about 700 of them by now—in many shapes and colors, including a few of the delightfully sociable double dulcimores. His instruments are beautiful to look upon and, what matters more, they "play." They play with a tone and ease that almost convinces the novice that he plays well. They play, I suspect, because they are produced by a craftsman's hand to suit a musician's ear.

For Chet plays the dulcimore too; plays it with a respect and enthusiasm for its possibilities that make the listener forget its limitations. He plays old songs, con-temporaries of the instrument, with a sweet simplicity of structure that matches the inclinations of the dulcimore. In other hands, the dulcimore cries out for the chords that a guitar can make, or speaks with resignation only to the melody. When Chet plays, the dulcimore makes music, dulcimore music that makes no apology and no pretense.

I first heard him play at a meeting and jamboree of the Ohio Folklore Society. He was on stage in a rather formal and pretentious auditorium, dressed in a brown business suit, one of his own dulcimores in his lap. He said very little—the dulcimore spoke for him, spoke of music remembered from childhood, of music all but forgotten, of tunes to pick and songs to sing. I have heard the instrument, before and since, in the hands of more learned scholars, of more talented (and sophisticated) musicians, and of more ebullient showmen. I have not heard it played with more respect and love than it got that afternoon at the hands of its maker. What Chet Hines brings to the dulcimore is a harmony with as well as from the instrument, a harmony based on respect for the past without foolishness or sentimentality.

Equally impressive is another creation of Chet's, the Mountain Dulcimore Society of America. Chet, I suppose, is President, since nobody else ever seems to have been elected; he may well be Secretary, and if the organization ever finds itself in possession of funds he will be Treasurer, too. One is tempted to say that the Mountain Dulcimore Society is Chet Hines, but that would not be true. How it would live without him is hard to see, but this loosely affiliated, enthusiastic, diverse collection of people interested in handmade instruments and homemade music has life and vigor and purpose beyond that which many better organized and firmly chartered groups can boast. A campout of the Society, with daytime concerts for the public and nighttime song-swapping around the campfire, is an experience rare in contemporary society. A group of an Appalachian farmer (bass), a high school English teacher (vocal), a long-haired college student (guitar), and a private music teacher (autoharp) is something to see—and their song-swapping from shaped-note hymns to gay-Nineties songs of sentiment is something to hear. For the Mountain Dulcimore Society Chet has been more than an organizer; he has been a teacher. He has taught the dulcimore, of course; but he has also taught that level-headed balance between a warm regard for the past and self-respect in the present. Now he tells me he is going to teach many more people about the dulcimore by means of a book. I am sure that the other, larger lesson he has taught so many will be in the book, too. Seek it out, reader, in the book and in the music, for it is a lesson of power and beauty.

George Herman, PhD.
Vice Provost for Instruction
Bowling Green State University
Bowling Green, Ohio

The Instrument
and Its People

I don't know where the dulcimore came from or who is responsible for its development and distribution throughout the Appalachian Mountains and adjacent areas. Neither do I pretend to have some secret insight into the past which allows me to draw positive conclusions about the naming of this delightful instrument—*dulcimer* or *dulcimore*. The latter is a phonetic spelling of the Elizabethan pronunciation of "dulcimer" and represents, more or less, the way it was and is pronounced throughout large sections of the Appalachian Mountains and foothills. I once met a young fellow from Clay County, West Virginia, who pronounced it "delsimore." I asked him if everybody in his area called it a delsimore and he replied, "Well, no; some call it a 'hog fiddle.'" All we really are sure of is that the Appalachian dulcimore was made and played by the mountain people during and following the Civil War. Other than that, the history of the instrument is lost in lore and conjecture.

I was introduced to the dulcimore when I was about eight years old. I don't really remember where I saw or heard one played for the first time. The beautiful liquid tones of the dulcimore are so much a part of my recollection of life in the southern Ohio hills that to try to separate them from other remembered sounds is nigh on to impossible. In fact, I'm not sure that I really want to—the cry of the killdee winging through the lower meadow on a hot summer's day; the drone of the ruby-throated hummingbird as it circled the morning-glory vines on the porch trellis; the urgent call of a whippoorwill from the front porch step heralding death to some member of the household; night sounds such as the hooting of the big owl in the giant chestnut tree on the hill above the house, and the cry of the fiddle calling all to dance (do-see-do and around we go!)—all these recollections mean "dulcimore" to me!

During the summer of 1935 I made my first dulcimore. It was a crude little thing made of hand-riven walnut with slats from an orange crate for a soundboard. Pieces for the back and sides were split from a seasoned log with a special tool called a froe, in much the same manner as shingles were made for roofs or "palin's" for picket fences. Good thin lumber was just not available to me, even if I'd had the money to buy it. The 3-foot log sections were stood on end and the blade of the froe placed near the center. A heavy wooden mallet was used to drive the blade through the straight-grained material, producing two half-sections with nice flat center surfaces. From each, flat boards were rived by placing the froe on the end grain about 1/2 inch from the flat surface and driving it through in a similar manner. These 1/2 inch "shakes" or boards were then reduced to about 1/4 inch with granddad's draw knife, which I was allowed to use on occasion.

The orange crates of the day were made of relatively good soft pine about 1/8 inch thick; they produced very good soundboards. We used orange crates for just about everything, from hauling groceries to storing apples and nuts in the winter. Anyway, the dulcimore made from these crude materials and only semiskilled hands was quite playable, and I spent many happy hours practicing tunes and rhythm patterns, even though it was little more than a toy.

My interest turned to other instruments, and as soon as I got two dollars ahead I bought my first guitar and, alas, set the dulcimore aside, reviving my interest in it only after considerable time had passed. However, since the late 1940s I have spent much of my free time making, playing, and studying the physics of the dulcimore.

The hours so spent have been consistently the happiest of my life. I want the reader to understand the dulcimore and recognize it for what it is—a "natural" instrument developed by persons who lived close to nature, and one that is simple in construction and playing capabilities. Dulcimores are unique in that they appear in many shapes and sizes, but all have many elements of commonality that distinguish them as a "traditional" instrument beyond question. I offer the reader the opportunity to copy my masterpiece which is the culmination of many years of study and the making of several hundred instruments.

Lastly, I wish to impart to the reader a love for the dulcimore, for it is truly a "love instrument"—as John Jacob Niles ("The American Balladier," author, composer of note) once expressed it to me, "dolce amore"—sweet love.

A romanticist could construct a good story of the invention of the dulcimore, based on what is known and reenforced by the absence of documented evidence. He could say that the first dulcimore consisted of a single string stretched the length of a section of a hollow log, and was made either to amuse a child or, indeed, the maker himself.

During winter seasons when inclement weather prohibited venturing outside, the father of the pioneer family indulged in similar activities. Hollow bones were made into whistles, flat bone sections were shaped into "bones" for rhythmic rattling, and drums and tom-toms were made of hollow log sections and leather. During the spring seasons when sap was "rizin," whistles were made of willow limb sections, "bull-roarers" were fashioned of thin slats of wood and a 3- to 6-foot piece of "whang" or heavy cord. The latter produced a loud roaring sound when the slat was whirled around the head. In the fall and early winter, fiddles were fashioned of cornstalks. Even in the summer months nature provided the pioneer's child with sound-producing devices in the form of "dandelion stem flutes," and various leaves that would vibrate when placed on the tongue and blown against in a specific manner. The vane attached to maple seeds produced a very shrill, controllable pitch sound when treated in this fashion. All these devices, as well as crude fiddles made of rectangular boxes not unlike the modern cigar box, were "field tested" by me during my childhood, by my father, and indeed by my grandfather!

It is not difficult to accept the possibility of a hollow log dulcimore devised in the manner and under the circumstances described when you consider the penchant of the pioneer for sound-producing devices (hence music) for self-amusement. He, of course, recognized from experience that shortening a string raised the pitch of the tone produced by the string, and his knowledge of modal music permitted him to play simple tunes very quickly to his own delight as well as those around him.

It is doubtful at this stage of development (if it did indeed take place in this manner) that the dulcimore could be related to any other instrument. As time passed, however, and the inventor demanded more sophisticated music from his "hollow log and whang" instruments, he experimented with crude chords and provided strings to play dronelike harmony, similar to that of the bagpipe. The assumed influence of the bagpipe on the development of the dulcimore is not difficult to accept. Throughout the British Isles, from whence came the bulk of the settlers, the bagpipes were prevalent in many and various forms, some of which still survive.

The bagpipe is a wind instrument that in its most elementary form consists of a perforated pipe, called a chanter, that contains a reed for sound production. The chanter is inserted in an airtight bag, which serves as a reservoir for air entering the bag through a blowpipe. The first improvement of the bagpipe was the addition of a second pipe to provide a simple drone harmony, and this feature is the chief characteristic of all bagpipes. The number of drones has increased from time to time, to a peak of six.

Early bags consisted of whole skins of small farm animals or the stomachs or bladders of larger animals. The mode of inflation was either the player's breath or small bellows provided for that purpose. The mouth-blown bagpipe appears to have been common throughout the British Isles and, in its improved form, is the Highland pipe of Scotland and the warpipe of Ireland. At least six other pipes have been known to exist in the British Isles.

In Scotland, the oldest known instrument dates back to 1409 and is preserved in Edinburgh. It has two tenor drones, a chanter with eight holes, and a blowpipe. From this type of instrument has evolved the present-day great pipe, with the addition of the bass drone about 1700. The modern Highland pipe has two tenor drones tuned in unison one octave below the keynote (a') on the chanter and the bass drone is one octave below the tenors. Occasionally, however, the drones were tuned in fifths, as were the dulcimore drone strings at a later time.

The Scottish Lowland pipe is musically similar to the Highland pipe, although the instrument is somewhat smaller. The drones were often tuned in fifths. This pipe was sometimes bellows-blown. The tuning of the Scottish small pipe differed from the modern tuning of the great pipe. The smallest drone was tuned to the keynote of the chanter; the largest, one octave below; and the intermediate at the fifth above it. This is a very good dulcimore tuning arrangement. Apparently the Irish warpipe faded into obscurity, only to be revived in 1900 by Henry Stark (London) and named the "Brian Boru." This instrument has three drones—a tenor, one octave below the keynote, and a bass an additional octave lower. The baritone is tuned to the fifth in between. (Again, the dulcimore tuning.)

In Northern England (Northumberland) several pipes were used. The half-long pipe is similar to the Scottish Lowland pipe. The three drones are arranged as tenor, baritone, and bass, with the bass an octave below the tenor, and the baritone a fifth in between. The Northumberland small pipe has drones similar to dulcimore tuning. This instrument has gone through a period of very active evolution, having been refined to a relatively high state.

In 1805, John Peacock and John Dunn, pipemakers of Newcastle, added four keys to the small pipe. Shortly thereafter a fifth key was added, allowing the pipe to play in an additional tonic key a fifth below the original key. At the same time, keys were added to stop the drones. Robert Reid of North Shields added further keys and by 1837 the number had increased to 14 and the drones to five. His son, James, added three more keys making the total 17 with a full chromatic scale from b to b".

And so the tradition of the bagpipe drone harmony among the early settlers can be established. Further, this harmony can be identified, in many cases, as a duplicate of that created by the dulcimore drones. There can be little doubt that if the drone harmony of the bagpipe was not directly translated to the dulcimore then, at least, the familiar sounds that were produced certainly influenced the *acceptance* of the instrument by the settlers.

The Appalachian Mountain dulcimore is, by virtue of its physical configuration, a fretted zither. The sound box is a hollow resonator approximately the same length as the strings, which are arranged parallel to one side of the sound box. The strings are pressed against low ridges called "frets." In this manner the strings are shortened or stopped at definite intervals. The spacing of the frets along the length of the strings determines the tonal intervals in accordance with a desired musical mode or scale.

The fact that the dulcimore can be placed in the fretted zither family does not necessarily imply a progenitive relationship with other members of this family. Fretted zithers have appeared in many remote cultures throughout the world. To assume that one such instrument was developed as an adaptation or modification of another, or that the instrument passed from one culture to another, when historical facts do not indicate a timely intermingling of these cultures is overly presumptive, to say the least. Of course, there were isolated cases in which strange instruments and music were taken to Europe from the Orient. For the most part, however, we must assume that this influence on folk music and musical instrument designs was relatively small. The fact remains that musical instruments were often developed spontaneously or with only casual exposure to similar instruments of other cultures, and this revolutionary process is still going on. New instruments of an electronic nature have been developed in recent years, using some of the mechanics of older ones. Once the instrument is developed to a practical stage and its virtues recognized, a long-range evolutionary process sets in. The instrument is either continuously improved and enjoys a wide popularity among its adherents, or it dies as the result of another major invention.

From the past we can see the spontaneity of the appearance of musical instruments within a culture. The Indians of South America are reported to have developed every type of flute or musical whistle known to European cultures. It is farfetched to assume that this is the result of some intermingling of the two cultures in the dim past.

Some time ago, maybe as far back as one thousand years, an instrument called a "citar" or some similar name, was developed in the area often referred to as Persia. This instrument should not be confused with the modern-day sitar of India. Frequently, names of instruments were borrowed and applied to those quite different in physical and mechanical design. This zither-like instrument, the citar, appeared later in the Balkans and was known by variations of "cymblom" or "cymbola."

Probably it made its way west, through the intermingling of cultural groups, to France, where it was returned to scales and modes less Oriental in nature—or did the French version arise spontaneously? In any event, the French version enjoyed considerable popularity in the 16th and 17th centuries. During this time the plucking technique was virtually abandoned for a hammer technique using small leather-covered mallets. The hammered zither was called "tympanon" by the French, for very obvious reasons.

The popularity of the instrument spread to the British Isles, where it was renamed. No doubt, the English were enchanted with its beautiful dulcet qualities, and drawing from Latin the word *dulcis* (sweet) and attaching a Greek suffix *melos* (melody), they arrived at dulsi-melos—*sweet music*—which was quickly shortened or corrupted to "dulcimer," pronounced dulci*more* by the Elizabethan English. It was in this form that the hammered dulcimore came to America with the early colonists and thence to the Appalachian Mountain area with the settlers in the 18th century—a trapezoidal-shaped instrument with from 30 to 50 strings played with small mallets. Many fine specimens still remain in homes throughout the Midwest and many more are on display in museums across the United States. In recent years there has been a renewed interest in this instrument, with fanciers building and playing some very fine copies of the old hammered dulcimer.

With the invention of the keyboard, which was applied to many different instruments with varying degrees of success, the hammered dulcimer became the "pianoforte," and hence the modern-day piano. This represents the pinnacle of the evolutionary process of this instrument.

With the early settlers in America came every type of folk instrument, as people from various regions brought little bits and pieces of their peasant culture with them. Among these was a group of fretted zithers introduced into the Colonies by the Nordic settlers. A dictionary-like description would probably suffice for all—an elongated box over which three or more strings were stretched, the length (hence the tone) of each being changed by pressing the strings against metal ridges or frets. The German settlers brought with them, or quickly fabricated from memory, the *sheitholt* and the *hummel* (hummer) in many variations. The Swedes had such an instrument that they called a *humle*, whereas the other Nordic peoples had similar fretted zithers called *langspil* (Icelandic) and *langeleik* (Norwegian). The instruments were, no doubt, being played in the German settlements of Pennsylvania as the pioneers who settled in what is now Appalachia passed through.

The settlers of Appalachia were predominantly Scotch-Irish—Scots who had lived in Northern Ireland for a hundred years or so. They were true pioneers. Their fathers and grandfathers had occupied land that had belonged to a subjugated people and, by the dint of hard work and abounding ambition, they carved a wilderness into thriving communities.

Down through the history of the British Isles, Ireland and England had been at odds. Several attempts by various English leaders to "solve the Irish problem" had met with only limited success. It was not until Queen Elizabeth I with a series of bloody coups so decimated the peoples of Northern Ireland that the land of Ulster could be dominated by the British. She died in 1603 without realizing the enormity of Irish defeat.

James I of England (James Stuart, James VI of Scotland) is credited with establishing the colonization of the land so recently wrest from the unfortunate Irish. Peoples in the Scottish lowlands and adjacent Northern England were not faring well at this time in history. Crop failures and crowded conditions and some religious pressures conditioned them to accept readily the offer of free land and religious freedom in the newly acquired Irish territory.

The formation of plantations and the colonization process were handled in a most businesslike manner. The Scottish lairds and English lords were permitted to lease the land from the Crown (sort of a Homestead process, I suppose) or to occupy areas for services rendered. Instead of transporting peasants to work the estates, subdivisions were leased to individual farmers. The poverty-stricken Scots were quick to take advantage of the opportunities afforded them. This was the first stride toward the development of the individualistic race that later settled much of the areas of Western Pennsylvania, Virginia and the Carolina Piedmont Region.

The first settlers in Northern Ireland brought families with them and within 25 years had made such a success of the enterprise that thousands of their country-men followed. Some, no doubt, married Irish girls, and vice versa. To deny this would be to deny human nature and the nature of the Irish people. Throughout their history they have, like the Chinese, literally absorbed their conquerors. (A classic example—the Norman French from whom we get such good Irish names as Fitzhugh, and Fitzgerald.) These conquered conquerors tended to become even more Irish than the natives themselves. There are many Irish names among the Scotch-Irish.

To assume that the conquered native Irish remained passively subdued and encouraged intermarriage and other forms of social intercourse would be in error. There were frequent sporadic attacks on the Colonies. The last great one occurred in 1641 and lasted for 11 years. In 1650 British armies under Oliver Cromwell effected a pacification that punished both the conquerors and the conquered. In spite of the annoyance of fluctuating policies of the English Government concerning religious freedom and harassment of the natives, the Colonies of Northern Ireland prospered for one hundred years.

As more and more lowlanders and English farmers came to the Irish Colonies, the result of privation and religious stress in their home land, conditions began to change. Land to lease became scarce and leases were not renewed with the original renters or their heirs but were often let to the highest bidder. Consequently, many of the early settlers were denied the right to land that they had learned to consider their own. The drought of 1714-1719 further heightened the stress on these, by now, ruggedly individualistic farmers. It was only natural that they look to America, "the great stopgap," for relief. It is truly said that "the seeds of ambition that were planted in Northern Ireland bore fruit in America."

The Scotch-Irish left Northern Ireland in droves, and by 1775 over 200,000 were in the American Colonies. The first immigrants arrived in 1717 and settled in Western Pennsylvania. Some of the new arrivals settled in the established communities and cities but others, possessed by now with a wanderlust, sought new lands to the west and south, and they formed a vanguard over the mountains after Daniel Boone's trek and followed Kenton down the Ohio River to settle in what is now West Virginia and Northern Kentucky, and later, Southern Ohio. To see these Scots, who had become Irish, then Americans, as wandering bands of peoples with a single purpose tied together with strong religious bonds seeking a common promised land, is, of course, erroneous. They were the first true backwoodsmen. Most of their movements seemed to be in small groups or as individuals; clannishness did not seem to be the order, though there is some evidence that clans did develop at a later time when families and groups became isolated. For the most part, the Scotch-Irish moved with individual purpose and integrated easily with peoples of other origins.

It was during these movements that the people who settled the mountains to the west and the south were exposed to the music of the Pennsylvania settlers of Germanic origin. (They later became known as the "Pennsylvania Dutch.") No doubt, a glimpse of a *hummel* or *sheitholt* (or a *hummel)* and an earful of the drone harmony was stored in some fertile mind for future use!

As settlements began to form in the Appalachian area, the amalgamation of the Scotch-Irish, the Scotch-Scots, English, and second and third generation "Americans" of mixed origin caused considerable change in the life style of each. The language and customs rapidly changed as a result of the social upheaval. The log cabin was borrowed from the Germanic people of the Eastern Colonies, dress styles were borrowed from the Indians, words took on new meanings, and place names were invented and freely passed from one ethnic group to another. The sense of freedom as the chains of bondage were dissolved created a race of people like no other in the world. Did that individual with the observant eye and ear pull from his fertile mind the appearance and sound of the *hummel* and set about to make one from memory during this period of social adjustments? I think so! The isolation during the next one hundred years served to allow a "melting down" of the reorganized society into a fixed, stable society that resisted further change and intrusion of foreign ideas. The society was "contented." The speech forms, mannerisms, and customs were preserved in their modified American form. It was during this time that the people began to form family groups or clans similar to those of the Northern British Isles. A "code of the hills" developed that governed the clan rights, and many a feud was carried on relentlessly because of some breach of this code.

The music brought to Appalachia was mainly music of the country folk. During their lives as farmers in their former home lands, their life styles were fixed. A youngster lived a life quite similar to that of his father and grandfather. Tools, food, clothing, language, names of objects, and music were passed from one generation to the next unaltered. When grandfather sang a song about a local hero or important place, the children knew of what he sang. When these songs were transplanted to the Colonies, however, they lost their meaning. Gradually the lyrics were altered, the style of the music was changed to match the lusty, adventurous life on the frontier. Often the general musical theme that was passed on to the next generation and the next was altered from a slow, throat-filling song to a lighthearted, lusty tune with near-nonsensical lyrics. Music without lyrics, such as the old Scottish and Irish fiddling and pipe tunes, quickly adapted to the pioneer style of living. The music became less stylized, the tempo increased, and the fiddler was allowed more freedom to vary the music from stanza to stanza. Indeed to this day, it is difficult to set to note those tunes—one is lost to determine which note is a theme note and which is an embellishment, or which variation is the original tune. One need only listen to the fiddle music of Eastern Canada, where the European style has been preserved, and compare it with that of Appalachia to see the changes fiddling style underwent.

It was during this period of musical (and social) readjustment that the dulcimore was developed. That it was invented by a single individual I have no doubt. Societies or peoples do not invent things or write songs or stories. These are done by individuals even though anonymous within a society. Some person faced with a need drew upon his knowledge and experience and set about to produce a musical instrument within the limits of the capabilities of his skill, his tools, and the materials at hand.

This person's knowledge of music can be presupposed; his life allowed little se in the form of entertainment. As to his knowledge of musical instruments, did he recognize the simplicity of construction of the fretted zithers of the Germanic settlers to the north and east? Had I been in his place, I would have. Had I only a "glimpse and an earful" I would have seen the mechanical advantage of having the strings supported by a relatively heavy member running the length of the narrow sound box, with no complex glue joints or stressing arrangements beyond my capability. I would have noted the simplicity of playing style, and had I the background of the Scotch-Irish and English, I would assuredly have incorporated within the drone string arrangement the sound of the bagpipe.

That our inventor was not thoroughly knowledgeable of the Germanic fretted zither is evident. The fact that he had no name for the first one he finished would certainly preclude an intimate knowledge of its ancestors. Some form of the word "hummel" could have been corrupted or anglicized to "hummer" or "hummingbird" (or you name it), but certainly not "dulcimore." It is true that the settlers were familiar with the English dulcimer previously mentioned (not a dulcimore), but why did our inventor usurp this name and give it to his creation when there is such a great dissimilarity between the two? Assuming that he obtained the name elsewhere, was it out of deference to certain church groups that he went to the King James version of the *Bible* for: "Thou, O King, hast made a decree, that every man shall hear the sound of the cornet, flute, harp, sackbut, psaltry, and dulcimer, and all kinds of musick, shall fall down and worship the golden image." (Daniel 3:10)? One can hardly object on religious grounds to an instrument whose name is taken directly from the Book!

That the instrument was invented and developed to a relatively high degree before spreading throughout the mountains, I have no doubt. At least the name was firmly fixed. Other than the previously mentioned "hog fiddle," I have heard of no other. The general flow of traffic from Pennsylvania was south and west. One could place the invention of the dulcimore not too distant from the German settlements of Pennsylvania—possibly in what is now West Virginia. In a short time the knowledge of the dulcimore spread throughout the general Appalachian area, indicating that the source was near a well-traveled route, such as the Ohio River, through which later settlers passed.

Dulcimores on Display

That the dulcimore is a relatively new instrument in terms of its evolutionary process, I have no doubt. The wide variety of shapes and sizes bears this out. Dulcimores are found that vary in shape from that of elongated violins to massive rectangular forms with double fingerboards. The sound boxes in many cases are nonsymmetrical, either by design or because of casual workmanship. The evolution of a musical instrument is quickened by widespread use and acceptance. The history of the violin (fiddla, fidel, fiddle) is a classic example. The development of the hammered dulcimore into the pianoforte, then to the modern-day piano, is another. The violin under the skilled hands of the Amati family and others took on a definite shape—one that is a compromise.

Notches in either side of the body allow ease of bowing, probably without materially affecting the sound. And the size is convenient for playing. The present violin shape is probably the best of a series of compromises. The violin is an old instrument, relatively, and has reached the ultimate in its evolution. Not so the dulcimore!

There is no such thing as the "dulcimore shape." *Webster's International Dictionary*, *Third Edition* (unabridged), speaks of the dulcimore (dulcimer) as being an elongated, violin-shaped instrument. This is true, but only in a very general sense. True, the dulcimore is usually elongated, but the rest of the description is too precise. I have seen some old dulcimores that were indeed notched at both sides like a violin, but I attribute that to the artistry of the maker—probably a violin maker who, on a one-time basis, decided to try his hand at dulcimore making.

For the most part, however, the resemblance of the dulcimore to the violin is nebulous. Many of the old ones resemble an elongated guitar. Others are rectangular or elongated ovals or some variation in between.

Some areas of commonality exist among the old ones; for instance, they all are elongated, with the body several times as long as it is wide. They all have a rather heavy member extending the length of the body. This member serves to support the force of the string tension, to hold the stops or frets, and to transmit the vibrations of the strings to the sound box or body of the instrument. This subject is discussed at length later. Usually, one sees from 12 to 17 frets or stops along the center member, which I like to call the sound bar because of its acoustical function. Almost without exception, there are three or four strings on an old dulcimore. However, the double instruments, which were designed to be played by two persons simultaneously, have a double set of strings.

These were often called "courtin' dulcimores" and were traditionally used during the courtship of young couples as entertainment. I suppose the idea that, "Those who play together, stay together," was somehow involved in this practice.

*Left: A Courtin'
dulcimore made by
Chet Hines for the
"Fat City" song group
(front view).*

*Right: Reverse side—
"Fat City's" Courtin'
dulcimore.*

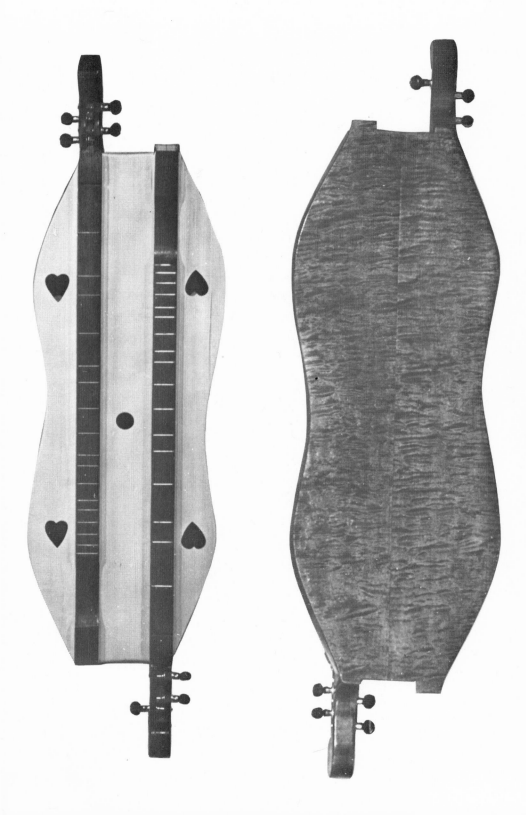

Among these several pages you will see seven old dulcimores which I present as a representative sampling of the many such instruments that I have located, photographed, and cataloged during my research activities. Each one is identified by its location with my catalog number.

RENFRO VALLEY #1

Of all the instruments I have researched over a number of years, this one is by far the most interesting; not because of its historical significance, as little is known about it. It is in storage at the Mountain Museum, Renfro Valley, Kentucky, in the custody of John Lair, entertainer, composer and for many years the producer of the Renfro Valley Barn Dance. There are no records to identify the maker or, indeed, the donor.

The general appearance of the instrument leaves little doubt that it is very old. Although the sound box is cracked in several places, discoloration and heavy warping due to dampness are not evident. Probably the cracks appeared as a result of over-drying and extreme age, as is often the case, rather than dampness or rough usage. During the useful period of this dulcimore's existence, several very crude repairs were made, the crudest being a clumsy attempt to reglue the junction of the sound box and the soundboard. These repairs (all made with the identical type of glue) would lead one to believe that for many years the instrument was not owned by the original maker or any other craftsman of consequence. The entire instrument was painted black, or a dark color that has turned black with age.

Often paint or a heavy finish on a dulcimore can disclose much to an experienced investigator. For instance, the fact that the repairs are made *over* the black finish indicates that the finish was applied early in the life of the instrument—probably by the maker.

(Photo by Howard Waker)
Left: Renfro Valley # 1—
Front view.

(Photo by Howard Waker)
Right: Renfro Valley # 1—
Side view.

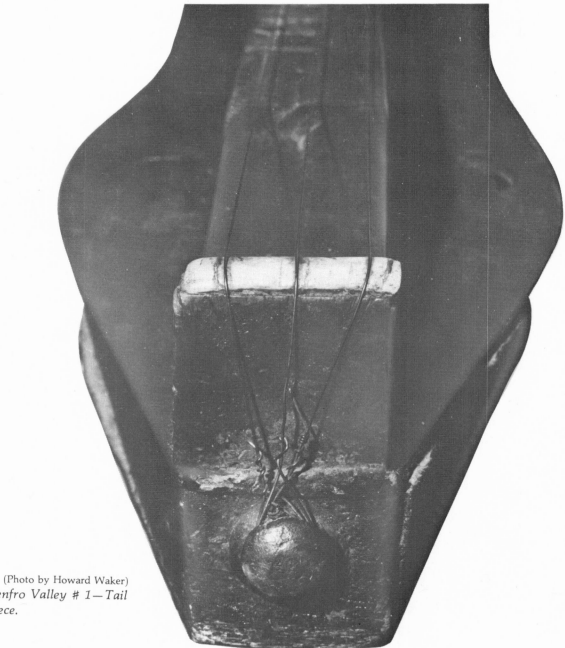

(Photo by Howard Waker)
Renfro Valley # 1—Tail piece.

(Photo by Howard Waker)
Renfro Valley # 1—Tuning head.

The owner was a frequent player, as is evidenced by signs of heavy wear at several points where the player would touch the instrument while playing. It appears that one player (or at least players with one playing style) made these worn places. This is substantiated by a heavily worn area on the right side of the sound box near the tail end of the instrument where a player rested his fingers when strumming with his thumb. As this method (which I use, incidentally) was not a widely used technique, it is not likely that more than one person played this dulcimore to any great extent.

The sound box, made entirely of maple, is 6-1/4 inches wide and 2 inches thick and is a classic example of the beautiful hourglass shape now publicly accepted (though not borne out by my investigation) as the "traditional dulcimore shape." The overall length of this instrument is 38 inches, with a string length of 29-3/4 inches between the ebony nut and the bone bridge.

The hollow sound bar is 1-3/4 inches wide and 1-3/4 inches thick, with 15 hammered metal frets on the fingerboard. The peg box is 8 inches long with 3 hand-carved pegs and an unusual scroll of a type referred to by one writer as a "Leprechaun's Shoe."

RENFRO VALLEY #2

This instrument is displayed in the Mountain Museum at Renfro Valley, Kentucky. The maker is not known; however, a close examination of this fine instrument readily reveals some of his personality traits and capabilities. He was a highly skilled woodworker, possibly a cabinet maker, as evidenced by the 1/2-inch walnut and poplar wood strips laid alternately to form a most remarkable striped soundboard. The back of the sound box is poplar and the sides are yellow pine. Neither wood is particularly good for the purpose for which it was used. Both yellow pine and poplar were used in cabinet and furniture shops, but were rarely chosen as woods for in-

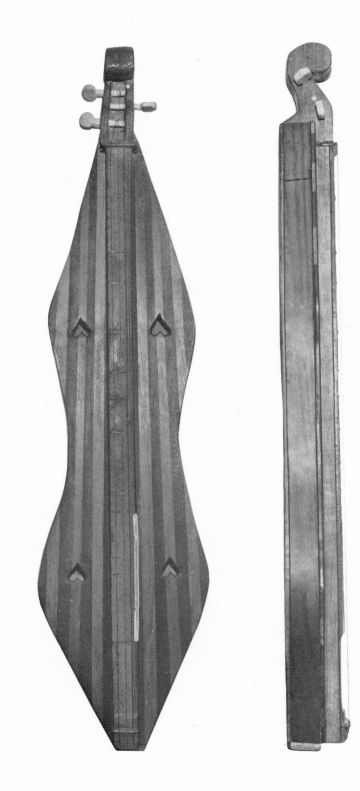

(Photo by Howard Waker)
*Left: Renfro Valley # 2—
Front view.*

(Photo by Howard Waker)
*Right: Renfro Valley # 2—
Side view.*

(Photo by Howard Waker)
Renfro Valley # 2—
Tuning head.

struments. The semihollow sound bar was made of yellow pine 1-1/8 inches wide and 3/4 inch thick, with a walnut fingerboard overlay to which 17 frets were attached in the conventional manner of their being bent into a "U" shape, staple-like, and pressed into two predrilled holes. The length of the three strings is 27 inches from nut to bridge, with 6-1/2 inches from the nut to the third fret, the keynote position. The sound box is 7-1/4 inches wide at the widest part and 1-3/4 inches thick. The walnut 5-inch peg box contains three hand-carved pegs and is terminated with a rather plain scroll. Sometime during the active life of this dulcimore an owner, not the maker, attached an angular metal guard on the sound bar for some obscure reason. The overall length of the instrument is 33-1/2 inches.

RENFRO VALLEY #3

"No. 79 Dulcimer made by W. C. Singleton champion dulcimer maker in Ky. Feb. 23, 1938, age 78."

The above information is handwritten on a small label inside the sound box directly under the left-hand sound hole of this instrument. The handwriting is of a Continental style popular in the United States prior to the early 1900's. The number would indicate that this, in all probability, is the 79th dulcimer made by Mr. Singleton. Whether he is a self-proclaimed "champion dulcimer maker of Kentucky," or whether such a title might have been bestowed upon him as a result of some contest or other is open to question. In any event, the instrument speaks well for his craftmanship in spite of the casual finishing. One can usually tell when an instrument was made by an experienced craftsman in his later years of practice from the sureness of knife cuts, the result of long years of practice; by the careful fit of the tuning pegs with casually carved heads; by carefully fitted joints; the casual cut of the sound holes; and by the often total lack of finish of any sort. Precision is the rule only if it contributes to the value of the piece as a musical instrument. Mr. Singleton's "dul-

(Photo by Howard Waker)
Left: Renfro Valley # 3—
Front view.

(Photo by Howard Waker)
Right: Renfro Valley # 3—
Side view.

(Photo by Howard Waker)
Renfro Valley # 3—
Tuning head.

cimer No. 79" was originally equipped with four strings, 28 inches long as measured between the maple nut and bridge. One hand-carved tuning peg is missing, however, and it has been restrung as a three-stringed instrument. Whether the removal of the fourth peg was intentional to convert to a simpler playing dulcimore, or was lost or possibly broken and not replaced is, of course, impossible to determine. The design of the walnut sound box is the simplest that could possibly be contrived, with the exception perhaps of the rectangular shape sometimes seen on cruder homemade instruments. The sides are bent in such a gentle bow that steaming or kerfing of the wood was not necessary. It is 6-3/4 inches across at its widest part. The sound bar appears to be solid walnut, 1-1/2 inches wide by 3/4 inch high. It is equipped with 16 wire frets arranged to produce a standard diatonic scale, with the keynote on the third fret 6-3/4 inches from the nut. The overall length of this instrument is 34-1/2 inches.

My copy of the Singleton instrument is one of my best dulcimores, which speaks highly of Mr. Singleton's skill as a designer.

LEVI JACKSON #1
"HARMONIUM OR DOUBLE DULCIMORE"

This type of dulcimore, although not in common use throughout Appalachia, can occasionally be found in collections or among family treasures. The double sound bar allowed two players, facing each other across a table or seated facing each other in a knee-to-knee position, to perform on the instrument simultaneously. One player would play the "lead" or melody on one fingerboard while the other "seconded" or chorded on the other fingerboard, which was sometimes tuned an octave below the melody strings. Dulcimores of this type are often called "courtin' dulcimores." They were reputedly used by young couples as self-entertainment during their courting period. In addition to developing "togetherness" as the young

(Photo by Howard Waker)

Levi Jackson # 1—
Harmonium or Double
dulcimore—Front view.

swain and his intended became proficient in dual playing, the music served as a monitoring device for the chaperone. No doubt, a member of the maiden's family would appear if for some reason the music were to stop for any length of time. Tradition has it that when couples could play well together, wedding vows would soon follow!

This particular specimen was located in the museum at Levi Jackson State Park near London, Kentucky. The maker is not known. The display card accompanying the instrument reads:

"HARMONIUM OR DOUBLE DULCIMORE

Given 1944 by Wm. A. Price, Corbin, Kentucky. Had belonged to Rev. Harvey Burnett of Somerset, Ky."

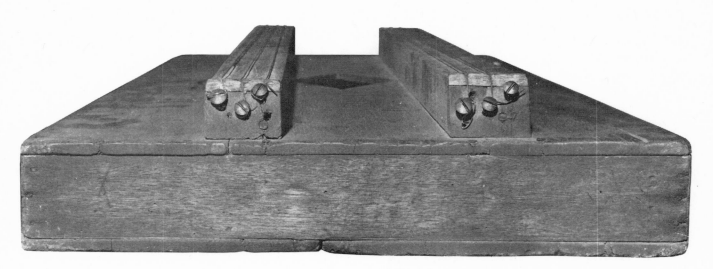

Levi Jackson # 1—Tuning head.   (Photo by Howard Waker)

The sound box of this instrument is rectangular, 36 inches long, 16 inches wide, and 3 inches thick. The entire sound box including the soundboard is made of 1/2-inch material of undetermined origin. The entire instrument has been treated with a preservative, which unfortunately prevents positive identification of the wood. The back or bottom (not shown) of the sound box is made in two pieces with a 1/4-inch crack between. It is reasonable to assume that the crack is the result of shrinkage due to the drying of the wood. The absence of fragments of glue in the joint between the two portions of the back, however, attests to the maker's unconcern for this part of the sound box.

The sound bars appear to be solid. Possibly a portion of the underneath side was chiseled out to form a cavity to lighten the sound bar, but this is doubtful. Normally when this is done, a slot in the soundboard is provided to join the cavity in the sound bar with the main resonant cavity formed by the sound box. Careful inspection of the inside of the soundboard disclosed no such slots. The sound bars are identical in size and configuration—2 inches thick and 2 inches wide. The string length (nut to bridge) is 32 inches, with 8 inches from the nut to the third fret ("do" or keynote position). Both fingerboards seem to be fretted reasonably "true." This would attest to the maker's skill or musical sense, or both. Occasionally one finds an instrument with frets so badly placed as to cast some doubt on the maker's sense of hearing. Each fingerboard is provided with three strings and 17 "broom wire" frets between the hardwood nut and bridge. Novel tuning pegs made of slotted bolts or wood screws allow the strings to be adjusted with a screwdriver. I will not vouch for the authenticity of these tuning pegs. They may have been added as replacements for the original pegs, which were probably of the zither or autoharp type, requiring a "clock key" type of wrench for adjustment.

LEVI JACKSON #2

"A DULCIMER

Given 1942 by Russel Dyche of London, Kentucky. Age not known, but it had been owned 40 years by Daniel Smith on Otter Creek in Clay County, who said it had been really old when he got it." (Placard with the displayed dulcimore, Levi Jackson State Park Museum, Kentucky.)

The sound box of this dulcimore is made of a variety of woods all 1/4 inch thick. The sides are of white oak and the soundboard, with 3/4-inch sound holes, are of walnut. The back is obviously not original as it is made of a rather poor grade of yellow pine. The shape of the back does not match the shape of the soundboard very well and several flatheaded nails are in each end to hold it in place. It is doubtful that the maker would have degraded his craft by using either the yellow pine or nails in such a fine instrument. A very startling fact is brought to light as one inspects the sound box more closely. The shape of the sides does not conform to the shape of the soundboard! Indeed, the true shape of the sound box is very plain, with a "false front" effect of the soundboard and a back overhang, producing the hourglass shape. Obviously, the maker intended to produce the hourglass effect for purely artistic reasons, but lacked the steaming equipment, inclination, or possibly the time to provide the sides with the complex curves to match those of the soundboard. The superb workmanship and artistic purity of design of the rest of the dulcimore leaves little doubt that the maker was a master craftsman and an experienced instrument maker.

The sound bar appears to be of solid spruce 1-1/4 inches thick, a rather heavy sound bar for such a small sound box. The 17 frets on the fingerboard are of broom wire bent to form staples, the ends of which are driven into predrilled holes. As the instrument was in a playable condition, the fret positions were tested by the running

(Photo by Howard Waker)
Levi Jackson # 2—
Front view.

(Photo by Howard Waker)
Levi Jackson # 2—
Side view.

Levi Jackson # 2—Tuning head.

of a scale, which was found to be quite true. This is not always the case with old instruments of more casual fabrication.

The length of the three strings from the bridge to nut is 28 inches. The peg box is 5 inches long, including the fluted scroll, and contains 3 hand-carved pegs. The wood of the peg box is tentatively identified as walnut, though a preservative finish, probably applied by the present custodian, makes positive identification difficult.

The tonal quality of this instrument is excellent in spite of the thickness of the soundboard and the sound bar. No doubt the fact that the sound bar is not hollowed out to increase the volume contributes to the excellence of the tone.

INDIANA STATE MUSEUM #1

This old dulcimore was located in the Indiana State Museum, Indianapolis, Indiana. I had the pleasure of renovating it for the Museum, and I also made a copy for their gift shop. The original is interesting in that it more nearly resembles a *sheitholt* with a small thin body or sound box attached than it does other dulcimores that I have seen. The sound bar to which the frets are attached is literally an elongated box, made of material that is the same thickness as the wood in the instrument's sound box. The overall length is 31 inches and the width of the sound box at its widest part is 6 inches. The string length from nut to bridge is 26 inches with 2-1/2 inches between the nut and first fret. Although the shape of the instrument is interesting and has some potential, the use of white oak throughout the instrument was poor judgment on the part of the maker. Had he used a soft wood such as poplar for the front of the sound box the instrument would have been much more playable. The craftsmanship is reasonably good. Close inspection leads one to believe that the maker copied an existing instrument without fully understanding the acoustical problems involved. The 17 frets are made of broom wire. Fret number 8 is misplaced by 1/8 inch.

(Photo by Howard Waker)
*Indiana State
Museum—Front view.*

(Photo by Howard Waker)
*Indiana State
Museum—Side view.*

THE HOLLY DULCIMORE

This beautiful dulcimore was built by James Holly in 1917 in Morristown, Tennessee. It is a copy of an older one that was made of sheet iron. Jim's father was a cabinetmaker in Morristown and contracted to make the copy. He then turned the job over to his son, who was learning the cabinetmaking trade. It is a large instrument as dulcimores go. Jim was able to locate the dulcimore a few years ago and photographed it in its natural environment. Judging by the height of a chair back (not visible here but in original print), usually 20 to 24 inches, the length of the instrument is 40 or so inches. The photo of the little boy in playing position (next page) also shows another old masterpiece. Note the tuning pegs apparently made of iron rods bent into the form of a key!

A James Holly dulcimore—Front view.   (Photo by James Holly)

On boy's lap, another Holly-built dulcimore. Note tuning pegs in instrument standing at left fashioned, apparently, from iron rods bent to eye-bolt shape.

Making A
Masterpiece Dulcimore

The accompanying illustrations show a number of hand-made dulcimores. Each shape is a representation of one made by an old-time dulcimoremaker and has its own tonal characteristics. In general, the larger instruments—those with larger, deeper sound boxes—produce much louder tones, with emphasis on the lower notes. Many of the features of the dulcimore, such as the shape of the sound holes, appear to be ornamental. There is no difference in response of a sound box with heart-shaped holes and an identical box with round holes of about the same size and located in the same place on the soundboard. Elongated holes and slots are a different story, however. They tend to serve the same purpose as *f* holes on a violin—that is, to free parts of the soundboard

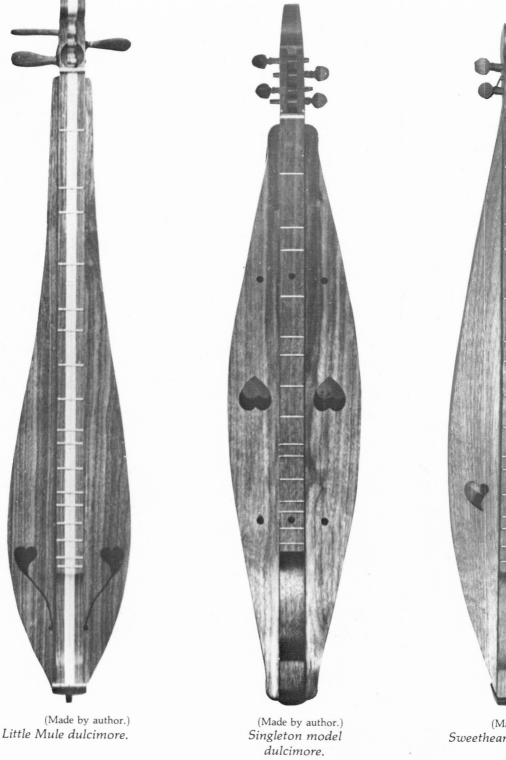

(Made by author.)
Little Mule dulcimore.

(Made by author.)
Singleton model dulcimore.

(Made by author.)
Sweetheart dulcimore.

from the rigid side members so that it can more readily respond to the vibrations induced by the strings.

I consider the large violin-shaped dulcimore shown on page 106 to be my "masterpiece." It is the culmination of many years of studying the building and improving of the dulcimore. The making of this masterpiece is described step by step. If you have a reasonably-well-equipped home workshop and if you follow the detailed explanations, you can build for your own edification an instrument identical to this one.

In addition to the explanations and illustrations, which will give you a good insight into the art of dulcimore making, there are full-scale patterns of the more critical portions of the dulcimore in the Appendix. Study the sketches and drawings thoroughly and become familiar with the shape and size of each part and its relation to the adjoining parts before you start to build. In purchasing materials get enough so as to have a little to spare when the project is finished. This is much better than running out of material just as the end of the job is in sight and, if some part must be fashioned a second time, it helps insure that the instrument will be of uniform grain and appearance.

SIZE, PATTERN, DIES AND JIG

As there appears to be considerable latitude in the shape and general configuration of traditional dulcimores, the shape of the one discussed here was chosen for its appeal to the eye and because it would reinforce the tones produced by the strings. (See Figure 1.) The size was easily established. The length of the strings (nut to bridge) had to be between 25 and 30 inches so that "off-the-shelf" strings could be used. A length of 28 inches was selected. The sound box was to be as long or longer than the string length. Because a semi-hollow sound bar with the nut several inches down from the solid upper end was desired, the box was made 33 inches long. As to the

THE PARTS OF THE DULCIMORE

1. BRACES   Internal braces are used to provide support for the thin wooden back and front (soundboard). They serve an additional purpose of anchoring the soundboard at predetermined points to control its acoustical characteristics.

2. BRIDGE   The bridge is provided to support the strings at the tail end of the sound bar. The height of the bridge is such that the strings just clear the frets when they are vigorously strummed. Its placement on the sound bar determines the string length. Small notches are provided in the bridge to accommodate the strings.

3. FRETS   Frets are small ridges fixed across the fingerboard. They are made of metal, ivory, bone, staghorn, or wood. When the string, which is at right angles with the frets, is pressed down, the fret tends to stop the string, thereby changing its pitch. Frets on this dulcimore are made of German silver and extend the full width of the fingerboard. On many of the old dulcimores, however, they were much shorter, allowing only the melody string to be stopped.

4. FINGERBOARD   The fingerboard is that part of a stringed musical instrument against which the fingers press the strings to change the tone. If the fingerboard is fretted it is called a fretboard or fretted fingerboard. Since the dulcimore was played almost universally with a fretting stick or noter and not with the fingers, the term "fretboard" is more appropriate.

5. NUT   The nut is a wooden bridge located near the upper end of the fingerboard or sound bar. Small notches are provided to hold the strings.

6. PEGS   Pegs or tuning pegs are small wooden or metallic devices used to vary the tension of the strings, thus changing their pitch or tone. Often pegs were metal hammered in the shape of door keys and were frequently called "keys." The wooden pegs used on this dulcimore are carved from rosewood to resemble violin pegs but are somewhat larger.

7. SCROLL   The scroll, as used in this text, pertains to the ornate, carved feature located at the extreme upper end of the dulcimore. Its function is purely aesthetic.

8. SOUND BAR   The sound bar is a device located above and firmly attached to the soundboard. The fingerboard and frets are attached to the sound bar and become integral parts thereof. It is the vibration of the sound bar, in response to the string vibrations, that actuates the soundboard. The vibration energy of the fretted strings is conducted mainly through the fret to the sound bar proper, hence to the soundboard.

9. SOUNDBOARD   The soundboard is the top or front portion of the sound box—that portion of the body of the instrument to which the sound bar is attached. Its function is to cause relatively large volumes of air inside the cavity formed by the instrument body to vibrate in accordance with the vibrations of the strings.

10. SOUND BOX   The sound box is essentially the body of the instrument. It is composed of the front or soundboard, a back of relatively rigid material, curved sides, and internal braces and blocks to form an acoustical cavity with a responsive diaphragm.

11. SOUND HOLES   Sound holes or roses or rosettes are provided in the soundboard to couple the vibrating air inside the body cavity with the outside air. An additional function of the sound hole is to relieve the soundboard from anchor points to allow for freer vibration. This is particularly true of "f" holes, which tend to free the soundboard from the sides. See Figure 1(b) for examples of sound holes often found on dulcimores.

12. STRINGS   The strings are thin strands, usually of metal, that vibrate when plucked. The frequency of vibration (or the tone produced) is determined by the diameter, length, tension, and density of the material from which the string is made.

13. TAILPIECE   The tailpiece encloses the lower end of the sound box. It serves also as an anchor point for the ends of the strings. The other ends are attached to the tuning pegs.

14. TUNING HEAD   The tuning head is often called a "peg box" in the literature. Frequently it is erroneously referred to as the "scroll." It serves the purpose of closing the upper end of the sound box and supporting the keys or pegs. Tapered holes into which the tapered pegs are pressed prevent slippage and subsequent loosening of the strings.

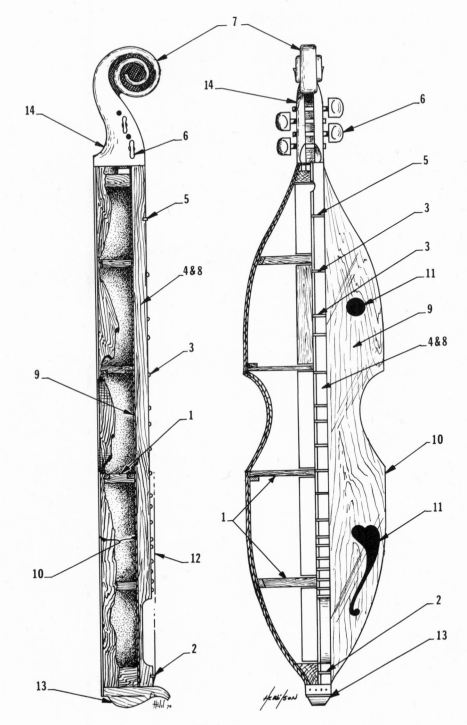

Fig 1a

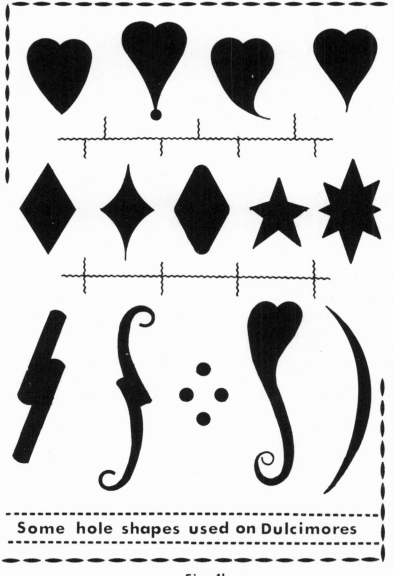

Some hole shapes used on Dulcimores

Fig 1b

width, the range is between six and eight inches for this type instrument. The volume of the box has much to do with the character of the sound (loudness, timbre, etc.), and for this reason the sound box was designed to what might be considered the traditional upper limits—8 inches wide and 2 inches thick (inside measurements). Many dulcimores are thinner than this, but the thicker sound box provides more volume and depth of tone. So the size and general shape of the sound box was established at 33 inches long, 8 inches wide at its widest part, and 2 inches thick.

The Pattern

Construct a pattern of building paper, cardboard or any similar material approximately 3 feet long and 1 foot wide. Fold it on its longest axis so that it measures 3 feet long and 6 inches wide. On this carefully draw the outline of one half of the sound box (see Figure 2). It is important that the two "S" shaped end portions of the pattern (from which the upper and lower ends of the sound box are made) be identical, since the same form is used to shape the side pieces that follow these contours. To make sure of this, cut a sub-pattern from another piece of paper and transfer the shape to the main pattern at each end. The center portion of the pattern that will form the violin-like cutouts are portions of a spiral, but might very well be made circular.

The next step: Cut out the pattern along the lines drawn. When it is unfolded, both sides will be identical (see Figure 3).

Constructing a pattern this way allows for a great deal of creativity without detracting from the quality of the instrument. However, if you are a woodworking novice or simply want to duplicate this instrument to exact detail, use the full-scale pattern provided in the back of this book.

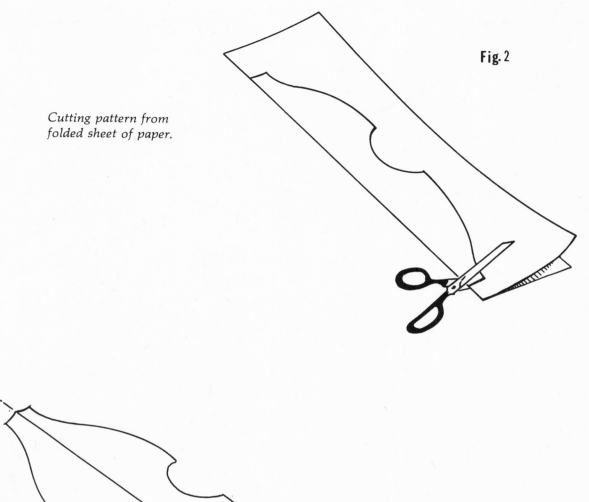

Fig. 2

Cutting pattern from folded sheet of paper.

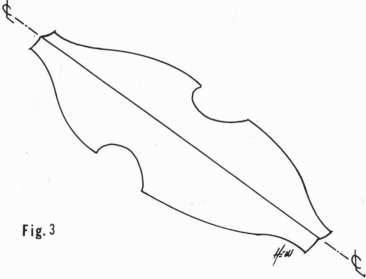

Fig. 3

When the sheet is unfolded after cutting, both sides will be identical. The exact pattern is provided in the Appendix.

The Side-Forming Dies

The sides of the sound box are made up of six sections involving two basic shapes—four S-shaped pieces (two on each side) and two curved pieces to fit the centers between the two S-shapes. Transfer these shapes from the paper pattern to heavy wooden material, to make the forms for making the side pieces. Cut these simple dies with a band saw and sand and rasp to match the pattern precisely. As there are only two shapes involved and the dies are re-usable, you need to make only one of each shape. See Figure 4 for finished dies with material and clamps in place.

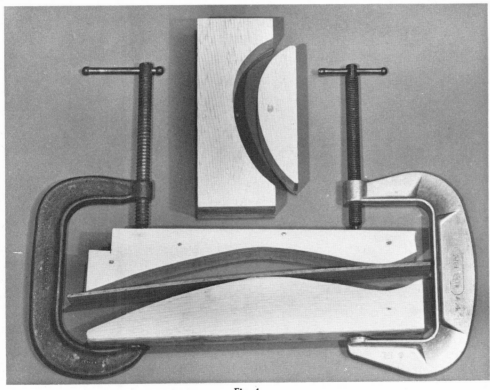

Fig. 4

Finished dies which are needed when forming the sides of the dulcimore.

63

The Master Assembly Jig

Make the master assembly jig on a piece of 3/4 inch plywood about 42 inches long and 12 inches wide. Glue the pattern to the board with its center axis along the center line of the board, placing it approximately in the center of the board. Drive fourpenny finishing nails into the plywood around the edge of the pattern to a depth slightly less than 2 inches. Space the nails about 2 inches apart, with room left at the ends and corners for braces (see Figure 5). These nails form the inside support for the sides while the instrument is being shaped, so it is imperative that they be set at right angles (square) to the plywood base. You will need additional nails to support the sides from the outside during the assembly process.

FORMING THE SIDES

If possible, choose a beautifully grained walnut piece, 1/8 inch thick, for the sides. Use oak, 1/8 inch thick, to back the walnut sides. As the oak is inside the sound box, it does not have to be particularly eye-appealing. It is readily available and responds to steam, which must be used to plasticize the wood. Occasionally 1/4 inch material is used for the sides and it is cross-sawed at 1/2 inch intervals to facilitate bending, as shown in Figure 6a. The 1/8 inch material calls for a different technique:

1. Cut the material in strips 2 inches wide and 1 or 2 inches longer than necessary to form the two basic shapes of the dulcimore sound-box sides. (The excess may be cut off before or during final assembly). It is well to stack the material and cut all 12 pieces to the desired width at the same time, using a fine-tooth or hollow-ground circular saw to ensure smooth cuts and identical widths.

2. If you make only one set of side-forming dies, repeat this step until you have a total of eight (four walnut and four oak) S-shaped pieces and four pieces

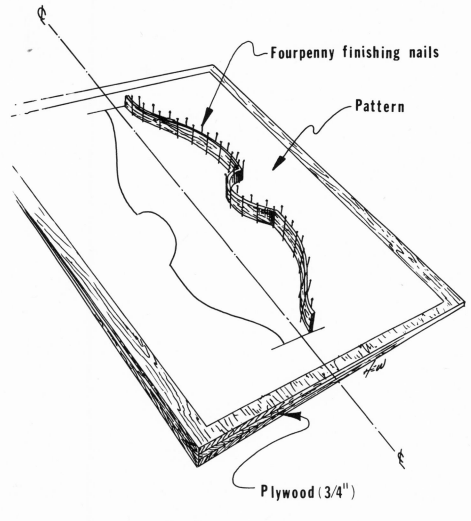

Fourpenny finishing nails

Pattern

Plywood (3/4")

Fɪg.5

The master assembly jig. This holds the side pieces in place during the glue-up process.

(two walnut and two oak) for the center sections. Shape two strips at a time in each die—one walnut and a matching oak backing. Use steam to soften or plasticize the wood. Place the strips in a pressure steam cooker for approximately 20 minutes. When removed they will bend easily and will have about the same degree of plasticity as shoe-sole leather. (An alternate method is to boil the strips in a large pan or vat for a half hour. This method is less desirable for several reasons. For one, the temperature of the water cannot go beyond 212° F, which is a marginal temperature. Further, the water tends to bleach the wood, destroying much of its aesthetic value; and the material becomes waterlogged, requiring several days to dry.)

Remove the strips from the cooker, using heavy leather gloves to protect your hands, and place the wood quickly in the proper die. Close the two sides of the die with "C" clamps. Make very sure that the edges of the strips are even. If one strip is crooked in the die, a messy situation will result and you might have to make a new part. Place the strips so that the walnut strip will be on the outside of the finished sound box. Now place the form in a drying oven until it is completely dry. When the formed sections are removed from the dies they will tend to straighten slightly. Taping them tightly together with masking tape prevents this to some degree. Repeat the process until you have the proper number of formed sections.

3. Now glue the walnut part of each section to its oak backing. Waterproof, plastic, resin glue, "URAC-185" manufactured by the Nelson Company is excellent for this purpose; it is available wherever materials for making laminated archery equipment are sold. However, you can use both polyester and epoxy resins with equal success. Spread the glue evenly on the walnut and oak surfaces in accordance with the manufacturer's instructions, and return the sections to the forming dies. Use "C" clamps to apply considerable pressure, which is necessary to remove the excess glue and hold the pieces firmly in place until the glue hardens. (The manufacturer's instructions should be followed explicitly.) Remove the excess glue with a damp cloth before it hardens, to preclude sanding and rasping. Here

Saw kerfs to aid in forming

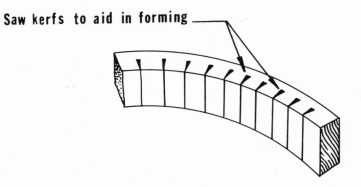

Fig 6 a

To facilitate bending ¼ inch sides to shape, saw in kerfs at ½ inch intervals.

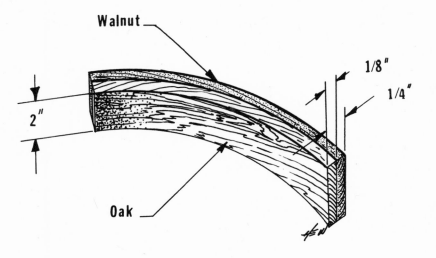

Walnut

1/8"

1/4"

2"

Oak

Fig 6 b

If using 1/8 inch material of good appearance for sides, glue it to an inner layer of 1/8 inch oak stripping after the materials have dried to proper shape in the dies.

again great care must be taken to align the pieces properly in the form. When the sections are removed from the form, they should retain their shape perfectly. Be careful, however, not to unduly flex the sections, as the wood can splinter and cause some difficulty during the finishing process. Repeat the gluing process until you have formed all six sections of the sides of the sound box.

Jigging The Sides

Assemble the finished side sections in the following manner, using the master assembly jig previously fabricated:

1. Place the center sections on the appropriate part of the assembly jig and adjust for the best fit. The sections were cut long to allow for this adjustment. The nails of the jig fit along the inside of the center section pieces. Since the eye is very critical of the instrument's final shape, be careful to adjust the position of both sides to assure symmetry in the finished sound box. If the assembly jig and the side sections are well constructed, there should be little or no difficulty in attaining a good fit and, consequently, a good symmetrical sound box.

2. Finishing nails are then driven in the jig outside the sections (Fig. 7a) to hold them in place.

3. The end sections must be cut to the proper length. When you are certain that everything is in place, mark the ends carefully to conform to pattern at the junction of the center and end sections. On the pattern this junction forms a corner as can be seen in Fig. 1 and Fig. 5. Remove the center sections from the jig and saw off the ends squarely at the marks. Return them to the jig and check for conformity to the pattern. If necessary, remove and rasp the ends until they do conform.

4. With the center sections in the jig, place the end sections (S-shaped) in place and adjust them to the best fit. Allow the ends to overlap the center sections. The end sections were originally cut too long and must now be cut off and mated to the

Finishing nails

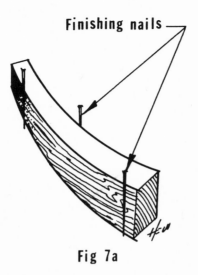

Fig 7a

Use finishing nails to hold the jig in place.

center sections. Mark and cut the end sections so that they just overlap the center sections at the junction of the two. Do this for all four end sections. Return the pieces to the jig and recheck for conformity to the pattern.

For the best appearance the oak inner layer of the end pieces should not extend to the outside of the sound box. It is removed in the following manner:

With the center and end sections in place, mark the *inside* of the end section at the junction of the center section. Remove and saw carefully through the oak portion only. With a wood chisel, remove the endmost portion of the oak. In Fig. 7b an exploded view shows the junction of the end section (upper piece) and the center section (lower piece). Hold all four end pieces in place using finishing nails in the jig outside the sections as in Fig. 7a.

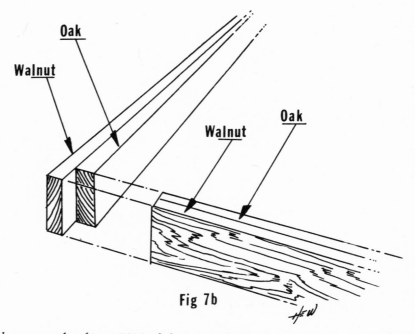

If the sides are made of two 1/8 inch layers, only the best (outside) material should be exposed in the finished job. Saw, sand, chisel, file or rasp as necessary so inner oak strip cannot be seen in finished sections.

Several words of caution are in order. The overall appearance of your dulcimore will be determined by the symmetry of the sound box and the careful fit of the glue joints. If the pattern is true and the sections fitted to it, there should be no problem with symmetry. The end sections should be worked and fitted one at a time striving always for a "best fit" observing symmetry as well as snug fitting joints. You should also be aware of the fact that the nails used to hold the sections in place tend to mar the surface of the wood. To prevent extra work in sanding and finishing it is wise to use no more nails than necessary against the outside surface.

Bracing

A good sound box should be well braced internally. If proper bracing is not provided, the box will not only be structurally unsound, but will not resonate properly. The science of acoustics applied to the resonance of a sound box is very complex, but the following guidelines are helpful:

(a) The back of the sound box should be quite rigid to reflect the sound vibrations back to the front; otherwise, the back will tend to absorb the sound energy especially when the instrument is laid on the lap as is the dulcimore. (b) The front is often referred to as the soundboard. The front of the sound box should be allowed to vibrate freely. It literally serves as a diaphragm or pump to cause the sound to be reenforced within the box—but it must not be permitted to move too freely, however. A reed will not perform at its best unless it is well anchored at one end, nor will a string sound its best unless it is held rigidly at both ends. (c) The sound holes should be so placed as to relieve portions of the soundboard. This will enable those portions to vibrate freely while others are rigidly supported. The shape of the sound holes is, as often as not, functional as well as ornamental. The internal braces should be so located as to not interfere with the positioning of the sound holes. The positioning of the braces is described later on.

1. Cut four pieces of 1/2 x 1/2-inch stock to 2-inch lengths to provide support for the junctions of the end and center sections of the sides. Then notch the pieces at each end to accommodate the front and back cross braces. The notches should be approximately 1/4 inch deep and 1/2 inch wide (Fig. 8a).

2. Cut cross-braces from 1/4-inch stock, 1/2-inch thick and long enough to fit snugly into the notches provided in the junction supports. The bottom braces should fit flush with the base of the assembly jig and the top braces should be level with the top edges of the sides of the sound box. See Fig. 8b for a view of the braces in place.

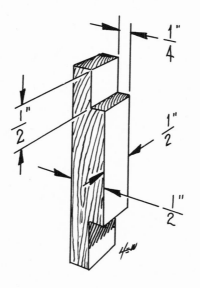

Fig 8a

Notching to form junction supports for front and back cross braces. This will strengthen the sides.

Final Assembly Of The Sides

When you glue the side sections in place, be careful not to glue the pieces to the jig base in the process. To avoid this, cover the base with masking tape at and adjacent to the points to be glued. Apply the glue in accordance with the manufacturer's instructions. Put the back braces in place and glue the junction supports. Use clamps to secure the supports. Then put the top braces in place and secure with small clamps. This is your last chance to determine the squareness of all the side sections with respect to the jig base, the fit of all joints, and the flushness of all edges and braces.

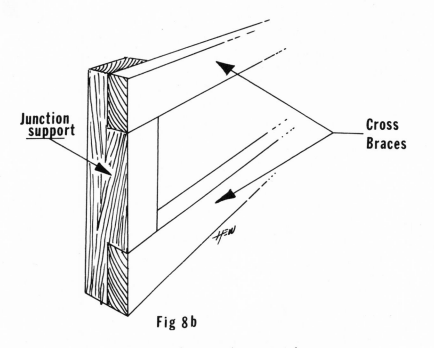

Fig 8 b

Showing the cross braces in place.

THE TUNING HEAD

This portion of the dulcimore functions mainly as a support for the tuning pegs which are used to adjust the tension of the strings. For the most part, the tuning head's size and shape have little to do with the performance of this instrument. The scroll is nonfunctional and could be omitted except for its aesthetic value. There are several rules affecting the mechanical function of the dulcimore tuning head that have NOT been observed by some dulcimore makers in the past:

1. The head must be large enough to allow adequate room for turning the tuning pegs—about one inch between pegs should do.

Tuning head—Masterpiece
dulcimore.

2. The head should be set at such an angle or the pegs so positioned that its particular string will not ride against pegs not associated with it.

3. The holes through which the pegs pass must be accurately tapered to match the taper of the tuning pegs.

4. The string slot which allows a coupling of the strings and tuning pegs must be deep enough so that when several layers are wound on the tuning head, the string does not rub on the bottom. See sketch in Fig. 9.

5. The side walls (see Fig. 10, Fig. 11b) of the string slot must be thick enough to provide a good grip on the pegs and not split under the strain of string tension or reasonable misuse.

6. The scroll, though it serves no useful function, should be well designed to provide for the physical and aesthetic balance to the instrument.

With these rules as guidelines, we may now proceed with the construction of the tuning head.

1. As shown in Fig. 10 the head is made up of 3 pieces of 1/2 inch walnut about 7 inches long and 4 inches wide to form a sandwich. If you choose to design your own head and scroll, a pattern must be drawn (observing the guidelines) and the outside shape traced onto one side of the sandwich. If not, use the pattern provided in the Appendix.

2. With the sandwich clamped or lightly glued together, cut with a band saw carefully following the pattern. Sand and shape the edges with rasp or power sander, as available.

3. Remove the clamps (or break the glue joint if the glue technique was used) and on the center section trace the bottom of the string slot which is the dashed line on the pattern in the Appendix. Cut along this line and the results should resemble the piece shown in Fig. 11a.

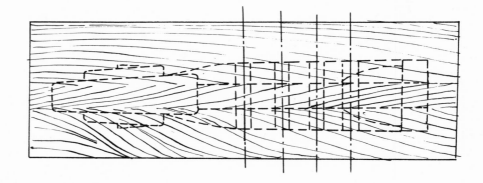

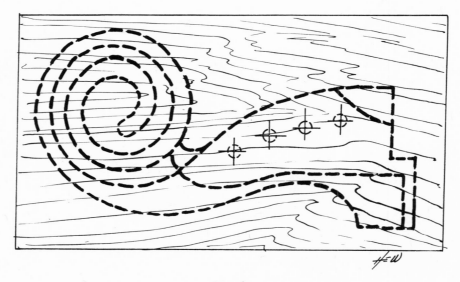

Fig 9

The tuning head pattern.

Fig 10

For the tuning head, three pieces are used to form a sandwich construction.

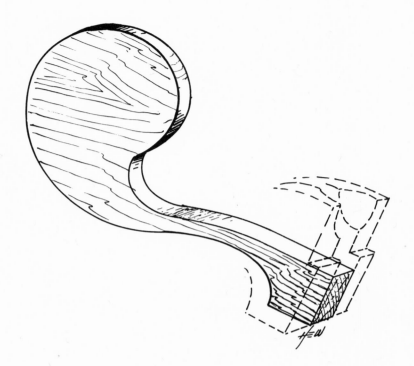

Fig 11a

In the three-piece tuning head, a special cut is given the center
section as shown here to form the string slot, described in text.
Refer to Fig. 11 for appearance upon final assembly.

If the three pieces of the sandwich were glued together at this stage a very nice simple tuning head similar to the one shown in Fig. 11b would result. However, if you choose to make a more artistic scroll there is more work to be done.

4. Place the pattern on each of the two outside pieces and trace off the spiral portion of the scroll. Cut along these lines and remove the freed portion. The sketch, Fig. 12, shows the freed portion as the shaded area.

5. Now close the sandwich, using a good waterproof glue, carefully fitting the three parts together with C clamps to hold them in place. As clamp pressure is applied, remove all glue which oozes out of the joints before it dries. Once it hardens this would be a difficult if not impossible task.

6. After the glue is dry and the clamp removed, mark the center of the four peg sockets or holes from the pattern. Drill 1/4 inch holes all the way through the sandwich. See Fig. 11b. (Reaming these holes to match the taper of the tuning pegs is NOT done until the pegs are finished and ready for fitting.)

7. The end of the tuning head opposite the scroll must be mortised to fit the sound box sides. Fig. 14 and Fig. 15 show the mortises in three dimensional views. The exact measurements and location can be obtained from the top view pattern in the Appendix.

8. Also from this view and from Fig. 13 the nature of the taper of the scroll may be obtained. Study carefully also the scroll on the dulcimore in Fig. 1. Cut and rasp both sides of the tuning head so that the thickness tapers to about 3/4 inch where the spiral begins. Then gradually taper the spiral so that its widest part is at the end near the center. Round all corners and sand to a smooth finish.

Tapering the scroll is difficult as no pattern can be provided. It requires very careful handwork and a mistake can result in it having to be done over again. An untapered scroll is acceptable, however, the tapering does add much to the appearance of the dulcimore and if you do a good job you will certainly win the approval of those admiring your handiwork and the instrument's value will be increased.

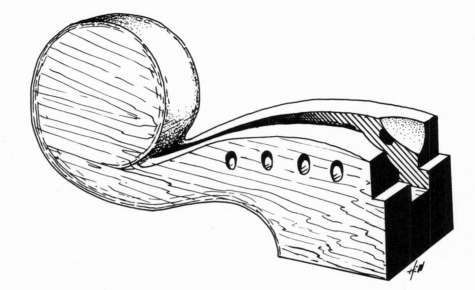

Fig 11b

The assembled tuning head, the three pieces glued together and sanded—unless one wants to use a jig saw and cut scrolls in the two outside pieces, in which case the head pieces should be only lightly glued (tacked together) for checking fit at this stage.

Fig 12

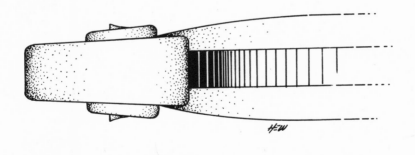

Fig 13

Showing extra-fancy scroll shape possible by tapering sides of head and scroll spiral. Top of head is made narrower than original head thickness (at bottom of scroll).

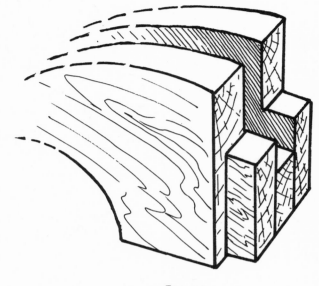

Fig 14

*One-quarter inch vertical notches are cut to join head and sides of
sound box securely.*

9. In Fig. 11b and in the top view pattern in the Appendix (also in Fig. 1), where
the tuning head attaches to the sound bar, the upper corners are removed. This is to
allow the strings to pass freely to their positions on the sound bar. Two methods
can be used to produce equal results.

(a) To produce a concave cutout, place the corner lightly against a 1-1/2
inch drum sander and grind off that corner until about 1/4 inch of material remains
between the cutout and the outside of the tuning head, then repeat this operation on
the other side. These measurements are not critical but care should be taken to make
both sides identical.

(b) An alternate method is to make flat cutouts using a wood chisel and, working with the grain of the wood, remove enough from the corner to allow the strings to pass. As in method (a) (above), about 1/4 inch of material is left.

The Tuning Pegs

A good material for the tuning pegs is Brazilian rosewood with a fair amount of "flame" showing in the grain. Many of the old dulcimores were equipped, however, with either ebony or rosewood pegs, either initially or by replacement at some later date. Others were equipped with either crudely "whittled" wooden pegs or, as was often the case, handmade iron or steel pegs. Some of these were simply rods about 3/16 inch in diameter and about 2 inches long, with 1/2 inch of one end squared to accept a wrench or clock key for tuning. A small hole was provided to hold the string, which was wound around the peg like thread on a bobbin or spool as the peg was turned. Other metal pegs were hammered out to resemble violin pegs, with flat surfaces to provide leverage, while others were shaped like, and very closely resembled, the patented keys provided to open sardine cans!

One can usually look at an old dulcimore, even one in a poor state of repair, and generalize as to the type of tuning pegs that are appropriate as replacements.

All these old dulcimores were handmade. Homemade instruments were, of course, handmade. A distinction is drawn, however, between the casual craftsman and the professional (such as a violin or cabinet maker) of the time. The difference between the product of the casual and the professional craftsman is evident in all antiques. In general, the home craftsman was equipped with tools that would be classed as "general purpose." For example, a sharp knife or piece of broken glass would serve as a scraper to both shape and smooth a surface—the shape and smoothness gauged by sight, or "eyeballed" in. "If it looks straight, it's straight enough." The professional—that is, one who owed his livelihood to his craft—was more prone to excel in terms of symmetry, surface condition, finish, etc., whereas the casual craftsman was mainly interested in utilitarian features. In general then, one can safely replace tuning pegs on dulcimores that appear to be made by a professional with pegs of the type used on violins. The dulcimore described here is representative of this type of instrument.

Cut the 1-inch-square rosewood turning stock to a length of approximately 4 inches. Turn a section 2 inches long near one end to form a tapered peg, 1/4 inch in diameter at the lower end and 3/8 inch at the upper end (adjacent to the leverage portion). These pegs can be seen clearly in Fig. 1 and photographs of the dulcimore throughout this book. Flatten the heads of the tuning pegs and shape to provide finger grips, and round the corners to give a more pleasing appearance. A pattern for the tuning pegs is provided in the Appendix. Four pegs are required.

Fitting the tuning pegs. When the pegs are finished they must be fitted to the tuning head. As each peg will be slightly different in taper as well as size, it is necessary that each peg be individually fitted.

Taper the four 1/4 inch holes in the tuning head using a tapered reamer. A violin maker's reamer is best but a 3/8 inch tapered rattail file may be used. The file is inserted in the hole and rotated counterclockwise applying moderate pressure inward. Remove the file occasionally and try the fit of the peg. Repeat this procedure until the peg extends all the way through the tuning head. Then use fine sandpaper to remove roughness from the peg and modify its shape as necessary for the best fit. The end of the peg may extend as much as 1/4 inch through the tuning head. Fit all four pegs in this manner.

COMPLETING THE SIDES

Now it is time to fit the tuning head to the side sections. First square and fit the ends of the side sections to correspond to the mortises provided in the tuning head

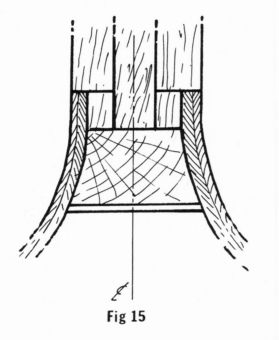

Fig 15

The tuning head and sides of sound box now joined together and glued. Note that a special block has also been installed to reenforce the sound box (see text).

(see Fig. 15). Fill the joint with glue and clamp the sides tightly. Be very careful at this point to assure proper alignment of the tuning head and the edges of the sound box with respect to the center line of the pattern. When the sound box is removed from the jig, the joint of head and sides can be sanded so that the edges are flush with the sides of the tuning head. The quality of this joint will be self-evident and will provide a basis for judgment by the more critical observer.

To further reenforce the sound box at this point, glue a trapezoidal block to the inside of the side pieces so that it butts against the inside end of the tuning head (Fig. 15). Cut this block from 1-inch-by-2-inch stock and sand it to fit. Hold it in place by driving a finishing nail directly behind it into the jig and wedging thin pieces of wood between the nail and the block to provide a tight joint at all contact surfaces.

Complete the tail end of the sound box in somewhat the same manner as the tuning head. Cut a piece of good walnut 1-1/2 inches thick and 2 inches wide and about 3 inches long. Make 1/4-inch mortises to accept the sound box sections as in the fitting of the tuning head (Figure 15). You can cut the excess material to an artistic "S" shape, as shown in Figure 16. Fit the tailpiece in place and provide a block similar to that used at the tuning head for additional support.

Now check the top edges of the sound box sides for flatness with a long straight-edge and remove any high places with rasp and sandpaper. This is very important as the strength and quality of the sound box depend on well-fitted joints and perfect seams throughout.

THE SOUNDBOARD

The soundboard is essentially the front or top of the sound box. It serves not only to close the sound box to form an acoustical resonator, but also as a diaphragm for pumping the air within the resonator. As we expect the soundboard to pump the air at an acoustical rate, we naturally use a material that responds well to the acoustical frequencies involved. The material must be thin and light and have a high degree of elasticity. That is, it should return to its original position quickly, with no appreciable tendency to remain out of shape. We refer to the proper desirable characteristic as being "bright." A "bright" wood is not heavy. It is not a "tough" wood such as hickory, nor is it "punky," as some of the lighter woods, such as white

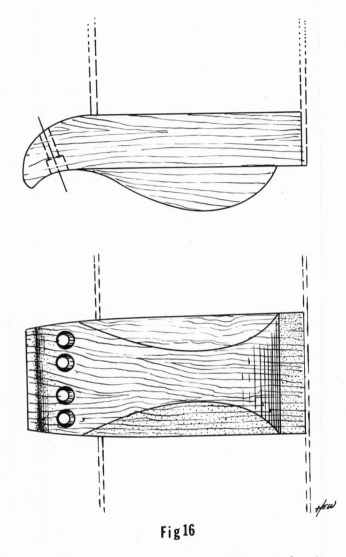

Fig 16

*If desired, excess material in the tailpiece can be given
an "S" shape as shown here.*

pine are. A good grade of spruce is considered "bright." It is light enough to respond to acoustical deformation, yet it returns to its original shape very readily. A banjo that has a loose head will yield muffled tones and reduced volume, whereas a tight, drumlike head results in bright, high-volume tones. This is because the tight head tends to return to its original position or configuration more quickly than one in the need of tightening.

A fine piece of walnut is admittedly a compromise between acoustics and aesthetic value. In the photograph on page 106 you can see definite striations in the grain of the wood. These hard and soft streaks appear to extend the full length of the soundboard. It is believed that the "harp string" effect of the hard streaks in some fashion contributes to the acoustical value of the wood. And, of course, the appearance of the finished instrument is important. As one is likely to spend as much as 200 hours crafting a fine dulcimore, he would naturally want it to have considerable eye appeal, even at the expense of a very slight almost undetectable amount of "ear appeal." This is particularly true of dulcimores with large sound boxes. As has been pointed out, the size of the sound box determines to a considerable degree the volume or loudness of the musical tones. For an instrument with a smaller sound box, one can expect softer tones, especially at lower frequencies. Therefore, the other factors that contribute to the volume and tone of the sound must be given more consideration in a smaller instrument, even at the expense of eye appeal—factors such as material used in the soundboard, the shape of the sound box, and the position of the internal bracing, as well as the type of sound bar used—hollow, solid, or semihollow.

It has been my practice to choose a size and shape in accordance with some preconceived notion and proceed to determine the best combination of factors to provide a "best" dulcimore for the shape chosen.

Make the soundboard in two sections with about a one inch space between them (see Fig. 17). This will correspond to the hollow portion of the soundbar dis-

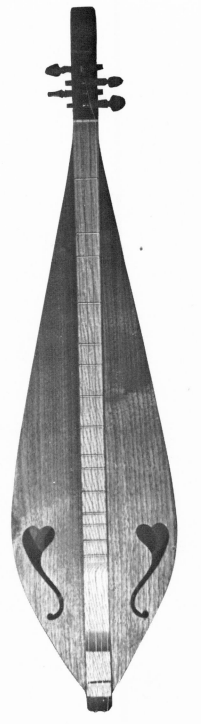

Teardrop shape dulcimore.

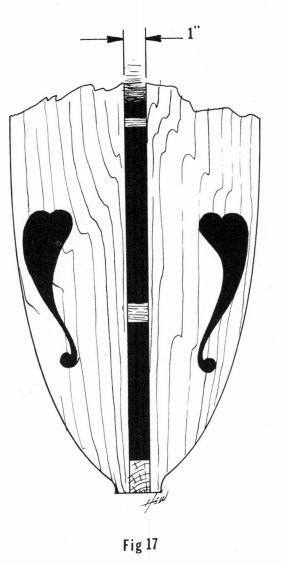

1"

Fig 17

*The soundboard is made of two sections,
the space in between them corresponding
to the hollow portion of the sound bar.
While this construction is optional, experience indicates it enhances the instrument's volume and tonal qualities.*

cussed later. Open construction of the soundboard is optional but tonal quality and volume of the instrument are somewhat enhanced if this procedure is followed.

With the two pieces of the soundboard clamped firmly in place and using a piece of 1/8 inch scrap material as a guide, draw all the way around the edges of the soundboard so that when the shape is cut the edges will extend about 1/8 inch beyond the sides to form a lip or overhang similar to that on a violin. Glue the soundboard in place and clamp or weight it firmly until dry.

THE SOUND BAR

The sound box is 33 inches long; therefore, the sound bar should be about 1/2 inch longer, because of the overlap at the tuning head (see Figure 18). The length of the sound box and the sound bar are, of course, arbitrarily chosen lengths. At the conception of this dulcimore the requirement was that the string length be somewhat shorter than the sound bar to allow the placement of the nut some distance down from the solid portion of the sound box. Most of the energy from the strings is inserted into the sound bar-soundboard-sound box complex at the frets—that is, at some point on the sound bar not rigidly fixed to the sound box structure. If the nut were on a solid structure the acoustical volume would be less when the strings are plucked open (unfretted) than when fretted. This can be easily demonstrated: first pluck a string open and then fretted, while listening for a difference in volume. The melody string is fretted to produce the tonal variation, whereas the drone strings are permitted to vibrate in an open or unfretted condition. The fretted melody string tends to sound much clearer if a hollow or semihollow sound bar is used. Indeed, on some dulcimores the emphasis of the melody string is such that the drones sound quite subdued in comparison.

If we assume that having the nut on a solid portion of the sound box and the

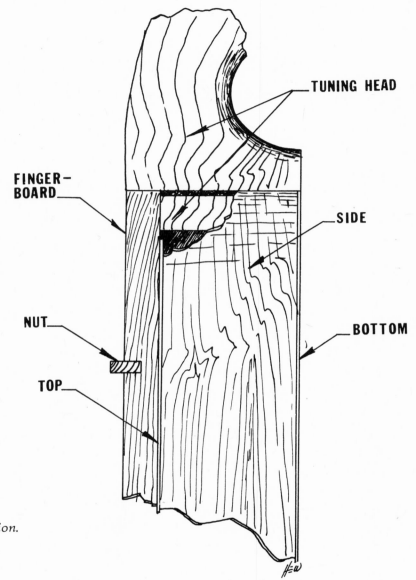

TUNING HEAD

FINGER-
BOARD

SIDE

NUT

BOTTOM

TOP

Relative location of parts—
sound bar/tuning head junction.

FIG 18

frets on the more responsive sound bar creates this unbalance, the solution becomes obvious. The nut should be located on the sound bar as if it were a fret. The nut on this dulcimore is located about 3-1/2 inches down from the junction of the sound bar and the tuning head. Drill a half-inch hole through the sound bar to provide further acoustical decoupling of the nut from the rigid tuning-head, sound-box junction. (See Figure 19.)

Construction

The construction of the semihollow sound bar is relatively simple. Cut two pieces 1/2 inch wide from 1/4-inch walnut stock to form the sides. Cut a third piece 1-1/2 inches wide from the same stock for the top portion or fingerboard. Cut the three pieces to the length measured between the tuning head and the tailpiece. To form the solid portion of the lower end of the sound bar (near the tailpiece) cut a piece 8 inches long and 1/2 inch wide from 3/4-inch walnut stock. This piece must be sandwiched between the two side pieces to form a laminate 1-1/4 inches wide. This laminate should be formed so that all three ends are flush. Cut a piece 1 inch long from the 3/4-inch stock to form a similar sandwich at the upper end of the sound bar. Apply glue to the adjacent surfaces and clamp the assembly in place. The resulting open-bottomed box must then be checked for "squareness, straightness, and flushness." Follow the diagram shown in Figure 20 to lay out the "strum hollow" or acoustical decoupler near the tailpiece. Cut it out with a band saw and smooth with rasp and sandpaper. The exact configuration of the radii at the corners or the slope of the cuts at the ends of the depression are of little importance other than aesthetic.

Frets

Probably some of the early dulcimores were made without frets, much in the manner of the violin or fretless banjo. The effect produced by such an instrument

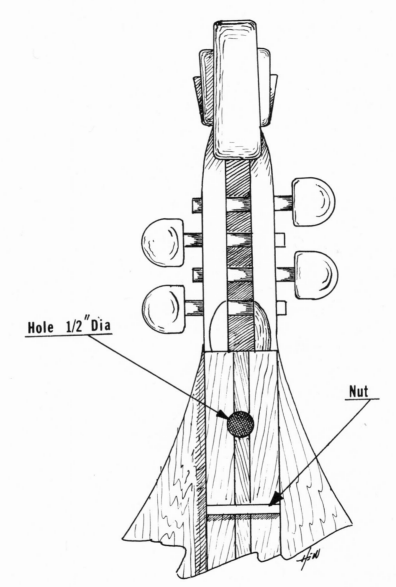

Hole 1/2" Dia

Nut

*Showing location of wooden nut
and ½ inch nut decoupling hole.*

Fig 19

is quite pleasing. The difficulty in finding the exact finger position is much greater than one might experience with the violin, however, because there is no "home position" or fixed reference point. The addition of frets to the sound bar greatly reduces this difficulty. It is necessary only to position the fingers or "fretter stick" in some relatively inexact position to cause the string to be held firmly in place on the fret, thereby changing the length of the string.

A range of fretting material used in old dulcimores ran from wood—either carved in relief on the fingerboard or glued into slots cut for this purpose—through bone, staghorn, and ivory, to steel, brass, and silver. Various alloys called "German silver" were also used extensively. Frequently, one finds handmade iron frets on early instruments. A close examination of these frets reveals hammer marks, attesting to the patience and craftsmanship of the maker.

Metal frets usually were made in one or two forms. Either thin metal strips were driven into sawed slots or wirelike "staples" were pressed into holes drilled into the fingerboard for this purpose (Figure 21). The latter method was the most popular, at least during the late 1800's, when wire from which to make these staples became readily available.

Often the frets on old dulcimores extended the full width of the fingerboard. Many were made, however, with the frets extending only halfway across. Inasmuch as frets were needed only on the melody string, the use of full frets seemed to be a waste of materials.

In recent years fretting material with a T-cross section has become commercially available. This material is convenient to use and the result is a very professional-looking job. It is available in brass or nickel silver with a self-clenching web on the "T" portion that is hammered into a saw slot in the fingerboard. This is the material used in the dulcimore described here.

The spacing of the frets on the fingerboard to produce a diatonic scale can be a tedious procedure. Fret positions for the just scale (scientific or untempered) can be

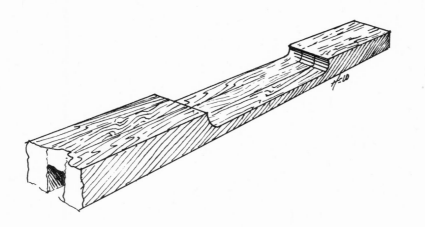

Fig 20

Diagram for forming the "strum hollow" or acoustical decoupler near tailpiece.

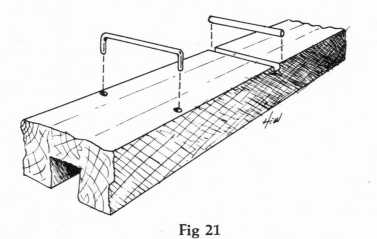

Fig 21

Either metal strips driven into horizontal slots or staple-like pieces of wire driven into holes may be used for frets.

calculated from the knowledge that the string length is inversely proportional to the frequency of a vibrating string. When this principle is applied for the just scale, the following relationships of fret position to string length are observed.

Frets	1st	2nd	3rd	4th	5th	6th	7th
L*	8/9L	4/5L	3/4L	2/3L	3/5L	8/15L	1/2L

(*Length of string, open)

This gives us the approximate position of each fret for one complete octave, beginning at the open position. Note that the 7th fret, whose tone is one octave above or twice the frequency of the keynote, is at the midpoint of the string. One needs only to substitute the string length for L in the above formula to obtain the approximate location of the frets with respect to the bridge. The string length of this dulcimore is 28 inches, so we would expect the first fret to be located at a position 8/9 of 28 (or 24.9) inches from the bridge, the second fret 4/5 of 28 (or 22.4) inches, etc., until the positions of each fret in the entire octave are produced. With a new length chosen to be 14 inches (half of 28), which is the length of the string at the last fret calculated, the formula can be applied to position the next octave. The author used this technique about 35 years ago to fret a dulcimore and surprisingly, the results were pleasant in spite of some dissonance with respect to the modern equal-tempered scale. This technique was later used to locate the approximate fret positions on fingerboards of several different lengths, from 15 to 30 inches. These fret positions were "tempered" by the comparing of the tones produced with those on a piano when the appropriate key was struck. The frets were repositioned accordingly. One could ask, "Why not use ratios derived from the equal-tempered scale, whose frequencies are known, to devise formulas for the fret positions more accurately?" The answer is that additional "tempering" is needed. On fretted instruments the string is stretched when it is pressed down against the fret, causing the tone produced to be sharp or a little bit higher in pitch than expected. Additional compensation is needed to correct this error. Even though we calculate the exact theoretical position of each fret, a noticeable error exists, depending on the height of the strings above the fingerboard and other factors.

The final solution, then, is to position the frets experimentally by comparing the tones with tones known to be correct. The fingerboard pattern used in making this dulcimore is derived in this manner. The fret positions as measured from the bridge are shown in Table I.

TABLE I
FRET POSITIONS AS MEASURED FROM BRIDGE*
(Bridge to Nut - 28 Inches)

FRET NO.	DISTANCE (Inches)	FRET NO.	DISTANCE (Inches)
1	25	10	10 9/16
2	22 5/16	11	9 7/16
3	21 1/8	12	8 7/16
4	18 3/4	13	7 7/8
5	16 11/16	14	7 1/16
6	15 3/4	15	6 5/16
7	14 1/4	16	5 5/8
8	12 5/8	17	5 3/16
9	11 1/4		

*A full-scale pattern for the fingerboard is provided in the Appendix.

These measurements presuppose a bridge height of just under 1/4 inch. The pattern is laid on the fingerboard so that the bridge position is about 1 inch from the tailpiece. The positions of each fret and the nut should be carefully marked in accordance with this pattern. Then draw pencil lines squarely across the fingerboard at these points. Carefully cut the slots to accommodate the frets on these lines to a depth of about 1/16 inch. A very fine-toothed, thin saw must be used for this purpose. If the width of the slot permits even a nearly imperceptible amount of movement of the fret, a "brassy" tone will result. In the extreme case, of course, the fret will rattle to the vibration of the fingerboard. Cut the frets from commercial fret stock and carefully hammer them into the slots. Round the corners and remove all sharp edges with a fine-toothed file. It is important that all frets be of equal height. To accomplish this, check the relative height with a long straightedge and hammer in or file off those that are too high. Cut the nut 1/4 inch wide and 1-1/2 inches long from 1/8-inch hard maple stock. Cut a slot 1/8 inch deep and 1/8 inch wide in the fingerboard at the appropriate place to accommodate the nut, and allow 1/8 inch to extend above (see Figure 22). Then glue the nut in place.

Cut the bridge from 1/4-inch hard maple stock to a height of 1/4 inch and a length of 1-1/2 inches. Unlike the nut, which is firmly glued into the slot, the bridge must be allowed to float. A floating bridge permits fine adjustment of the string length to further "temper" the musical scale produced. This procedure is discussed later.

Then glue the completed sound bar in place with care to assure contact with the soundboard and proper alignment with the tuning head and the tailpiece.

THE BACK OF THE SOUND BOX

To complete the sound box, choose a piece of 1/8-inch walnut stock somewhat larger than the dulcimore, for the back or bottom. Place the walnut piece on a smooth surface. With the dulcimore positioned on it, draw the outline of the sound box, allowing about 1/8 inch to form a head or overhanging lip as on the sound box top or soundboard. Cut the walnut piece with a band saw according

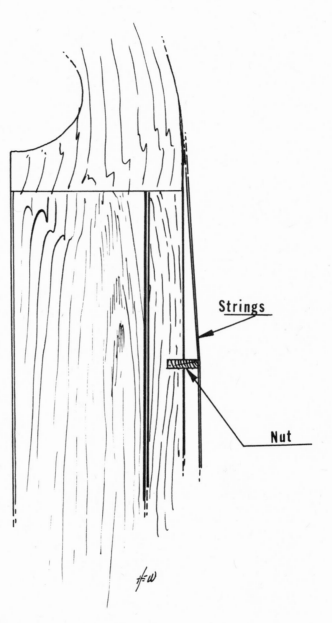

Strings

Nut

Cross-section showing
installation of wooden nut.

Fig 22

to the inscribed outline, and sand the edges smooth. Apply glue to all edges and braces of the sound box that make contact with the back. Place the dulcimore very carefully in the center of the newly cut back and weight it in place. Excess glue that flows out of the joints must be removed immediately. When the glue has set and the weights are removed, the edges should be further shaped and smoothed with rasp and sandpaper.

STRINGING THE INSTRUMENT

At this point the instrument is essentially complete. Before proceeding with the wood finishing, mount the strings and test the instrument (i.e., the bridge and nut heights, fret alignments, etc.) on the premise that it is better to make whatever adjustments are necessary before the finish is applied. To do this, drill four small holes through the tailpiece, as in Figure 23. Also, drill small holes through the tuning pegs to accommodate the strings. Cut equally spaced notches in the bridge and nut to prevent side slippage of the strings as they are tightened. In performing the last operation, avoid cutting too deep. If the strings are too close to the frets, they will not clear properly when plucked. It is better to start with the strings a bit on the high side and lower them gradually. Use three 0.012-inch diameter steel strings on this dulcimore (first or second strings from a 12-string guitar), and one 0.022-inch wound steel string (third from a 12-string guitar). As the instrument is laid on a table with the tuning head to your left hand, the largest string (0.022-inch) is the first string (Figure 1) and is farthest from the body. The other three strings, all of equal size, are located in the three remaining string positions.

Thread the first string (that is, the one farthest from you) through the appropriate hole in the tailpiece, over the bridge and nut, and through the hole in the uppermost tuning peg. Turn the peg counterclockwise until the string is tight. Install the

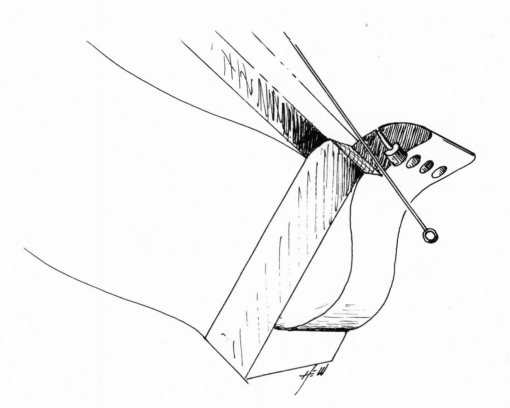

Fig 23

The first of the four holes made in the tailpiece to accept the strings
is shown here in cross-section.

second string in a like manner, using the *third* tuning peg. String the third string to the fourth peg and the fourth string to the second peg. (See Figure 1.) This arrangement positions the strings so that they tend to pull the tuning pegs into the holes, thereby wedging them more tightly as greater pressure is applied by futher tightening the strings.

Draw the strings reasonably tight, and individually pluck them vigorously to test the clearance of the string with respect to the frets and to ensure that the string is properly seated at the bridge and nut. A rattling sound indicates that the strings are clashing against the frets. If the tone produced is muffled and lacks brilliance, the string is not seated at the bridge or nut, or some small amount of material at the string notch is interfering with the vibration of the string.

Lower the strings at the nut by cutting the notches deeper to the minimum height consistent with fret clearance. This height should be just a fraction more than the height of a fret. The string height at the bridge is critical. It should be, of course, as low as possible consistent with proper fret clearance. One cannot rely on an open string test, however, to determine the proper clearance. The string-fret clearance must be checked at each fret. Starting with one string depressed at the first fret (see Figure 1) observe the clearance of the string at the second fret; at the second fret, the clearance at the third fret, etc. The third fret clearance (when the string is depressed at the second fret) is the most critical. This position is often used as a quick test of the bridge height, on the assumption that if the string is as low as possible consistent with proper clearance at this point and if the frets are properly leveled, no further adjustment should be necessary. Each string should then be adjusted in a similar manner, with particular attention given to the fourth or melody string. This is the string that the melody is usually played on and is the only string fretted in most styles of playing. This is discussed later.

The next operation is to adjust the bridge so that the string length is optimum with respect to the fingerboard. Remember that the string stretches slightly when depressed. The greater the depression the greater the stretch, and the *sharper* the tone will tend to be. Just as the string height was adjusted experimentally, so the length must be adjusted experimentally to compensate for any discrepancies noted. This is done by a process called "halving the errors." This process assumes that if the error at the midpoint of the fingerboard were reduced to zero, the error on either half of the fingerboard would be reduced by at least one half. Whether this is true depends on the care with which the fingerboard was constructed. This process consists of the following steps:

1. Locate the midpoint of the string. Do this by placing a finger lightly on the string and plucking it repeatedly. You will note that the tone is quite muffled. By moving the finger up and down the string, a point may be found at which the tone is much clearer. This occurs at the midpoint of the string. Note also that this point is just below or to the right of the seventh fret, which is the first note of the second octave.

2. Press the string behind the seventh fret so that a firm contact is made between the fret and the string. This should produce a tone that is identical with the tone produced in step No. 1.

3. If there is a difference, and if the fretted tone is too high, move the bridge to the right (toward the tailpiece). If the tone at the fret is too low, move the bridge to the left to shorten the string.

4. Repeat steps 1, 2, and 3 until the two tones are identical.

FINISHING THE DULCIMORE

When one is working with fine-quality wood, the question always arises, how should it be finished? Should the grain be filled? Should a stain be used? A sealer?

Should it be varnished, lacquered, oil finished? How about wax? The answer, of course, is that it depends on the wood (type, grain, etc.) and the effect desired. No doubt many homemade dulcimores were left entirely without finish other than the polishing effect of constant usage and the darkening effect of time. Good walnut responds particularly well to this treatment. Some old dulcimores have been subjected to long hours of hand rubbing with linseed oil. Others have a beautiful violin varnish finish, obviously applied by a cabinetmaker or musical instrument craftsman, as is usually evident in the superb workmanship of the total instrument.

The following conditions should be satisfied:

1. The finish must not hide the natural beauty of the carefully selected wood.

2. The finish must be smooth and professional looking, without a high gloss or an appearance of having been "overly finished."

3. A durable finish similar in appearance to that produced by hand rubbing is desired. A hand-rubbed finish is produced by the rubbing of the surface with the palm of the hand (a piece of smooth leather is often used), either with or without oil or wax, until it is perfectly smooth. If oil or wax is used, layer after layer must be rubbed into the pores of the wood until they are completely filled. Needless to say, this requires long hours of patient labor. You can save much of the labor by first sealing the pores of the wood with a good commercial sealer. Then apply the wax to produce a beautiful, hand-rubbed finish.

In finishing your dulcimore, avoid the use of stains or stain-bearing sealers. Good walnut has a natural beauty in the variation of its shades and tones of color that cannot be improved by the use of stains. Often a clear sealer will tend to accentuate these variations, thereby enhancing the natural beauty of the wood.

Finish the dulcimore in the following manner:

1. Remove the strings, tuning pegs, and bridge. Make a light pencil mark to locate the position of the bridge.

2. Then sand the entire instrument with fine garnet paper until all irregularities in the surface are removed and the wood takes on a light shine.

3. Clean the surface of dust by rubbing with a clean dry cloth, paying particular attention to cracks and crevices that might hold small amounts of dust.

4. Then apply a clear sealer to the entire surface in accordance with the manufacturer's instructions and let it dry. Two coats are necessary.

5. Then apply rubbing wax to produce the desired effect. Take care to avoid waxing the tuning peg holes. The shafts of the tuning pegs should be left unfinished.

Replace the strings, tuning pegs, and bridge to complete the dulcimore. You will be justly proud of it!

Author with his "Masterpiece" dulcimore—daughters Patsy (left) and Carole (right).

Making
Mountain Music

Assuming that you have built a masterpiece dulcimore in accordance with the instructions in the previous section (and the Appendix), or that you have taken the easy way out and have purchased a reasonably good four-stringed instrument from one of the several dulcimoremakers in the country, you are, no doubt, anxious to play it. To show you how, the following material is arranged in as simple and readable a fashion as possible. It is not easy reading, of course, being intended mainly for instructional purposes. A complete dulcimore "Lesson Book" would be voluminous and should contain numerous practice exercises and a full repertoire of tunes. This is not such a book, but it is complete enough to get you started. However, there is much more to learn about dulcimore playing.

Follow the instructions explicitly. If the information provided seems to conflict with that obtained from other sources, so be it. You must at the very outset adopt a method and rigidly adhere to it until you have fully mastered it—then, and only then, should you look afield for other methods and styles. Works by Howard Mitchell, John Putnam, and Jean Ritchie (the "Grand Lady of the Dulcimore") are available. Each author presents his material in his own style and, in essence, there is no real conflict. The consensus is that first one must learn simple playing techniques and simple tunes, and then fully master these techniques and tunes until the strings and fingerboard are no longer a mystery. This plateau can only be attained by methodical and diligent practice.

This method is basic. You start with simple, familiar tunes that can be sung or hummed. You learn that each syllable of the lyrics has a tone assigned to it represented by a fret number, and that a combination of a number of these tones, properly accented, makes up a musical phrase that corresponds to a single line of the lyrics. You practice each line until you have fully mastered it, then move on to the next line, master that, combine the two, etc. In the process you become familar with the fingerboard to the extent that "counting the frets" quickly becomes unnecessary. Hopefully, at some later time, reference to fret numbers for familiar tunes will no longer be necessary. At this point you are starting to "play by ear." For those persons who never reach this state or who choose to play by note, a technique for converting sheet music to tablature form is presented. Later, and again hopefully, tablaturization can be dispensed with, and you can begin to play by rote, automatically transposing the music to the key in which the dulcimore is tuned!

This basic dulcimore method offers a serendipity in that the student is *making music* from the very beginning. There are no long periods of finger exercises or "learning the basic chords" as is required in learning other stringed instruments. Frequently as the student progresses, his natural sense of rhythm will demand that he embellish his playing with additional strokes, especially between musical phrases (lines or the lyrics). He will sense that the drone strings need to be busy even though the melody is at rest, or a single note be held between lines of the lyrics, as is often the case, and he will add strums or other original innovations. In this fashion, a style is developed that is individualistic, satisfying to the player, and pleasant to the listener.

As the student (at this stage he is a dulcimore *player* though still a student) progresses, he will be tempted to experiment with other picking or strumming techniques. If he has a background of banjo or classic guitar playing, he will tend to adapt these methods to his dulcimore playing. It would be wise for him to obtain a copy of Howard Mitchell's very excellent recording and booklet in which various techniques are demonstrated. The quill technique used by Jean Ritchie, and others who have adhered more rigidly to traditional playing methods, also should be explored. Listening to these artists play the dulcimore, each using his own technique, is an educational as well as an extremely emotional experience. The student should be again warned, however, against jumping from one technique to another without fully mastering the first. One also must be on guard against feelings of inadequacy when listening to the masters. Remember, the dulcimore is played for enjoyment. The ease with which it can be learned permits a student to become a master if he proceeds in an orderly fashion. The tablature as a teaching method is not original. Many variations have been developed during the past one thousand years or so. Fifteenth and sixteenth-century meistersingers and troubadours concocted tablatures and sets of rules for teaching the lute and other instruments of the time. Indeed, this form of musical notation ultimately led to the modern staff and note system.

Further, this is not the only method one could use to learn to play the dulci-more. There is no substitute for private tutoring. The student can observe the movements of the teacher's hands, hear the sounds produced, and obtain on-the-spot guidance during the period of learning the basic mechanics of playing. However, the simple tablature can be of considerable assistance to the beginner while he is developing manual dexterity and familiarizing himself with the dulcimore. Later on, when the student can produce any rhythmic pattern presented herein, at least three directions are open to him. He may, by following the procedure for extracting the required information from sheet music, formulate his own tablature; go directly to single-line sheet music, which is particularly recommended for the more accomplish-ed musician; or he may utilize the dexterity developed as a result of his work with tablatures and a God-given sense of tone and rhythm to "go off on his own" and, with the dulcimore as a substitute for his voice, play melodies that are familiar to him in the best free-style dulcimore tradition. The last approach is the dream of most dulcimore aspirants. Each visualizes himself as a potential Howard Mitchell, weaving simple but beautiful melodies with intricate finger-picking patterns in the style of the classic guitarist — or a Jean Ritchie, whose beautiful quill technique causes the music to flow from the dulcimore like clear, cool water from a mountain spring!

TUNING AND PLAYING FROM LYRICS

The dulcimore is usually played on a table or across the lap with tuning pegs on player's left (figure 24). The string closest to the player (the fourth) is the melody string; the other three are "drones" or harmony strings. First, the dulcimore must be tuned. Do this by adjusting the string farthest from the body (first string) to middle C, if a piano or pitch pipe is available, or to a tone in the middle range of the player's singing voice when without other reference. The string is plucked with the finger

Fig 24 *The dulcimore is usually played on a table or across the lap with tuning pegs on player's left. (Instrument shown was made by author.)*

of the right hand and the appropriate peg is turned to tighten or loosen the string as necessary. When the string is adjusted to the proper pitch, a little pressure, forcing the peg inward, should prevent it from slipping. If it continues to slip when moderate pressure is applied, place a drop of water on the peg shaft, the part that fits in the hole. Sometimes it is necessary to rub a little violin rosin on the shaft to give a better "grip." The second string must now be tuned. Press down the previously tuned C string firmly, at the fourth fret (fourth from scroll) so that when the string is plucked it will respond with a nice clear tone but considerably higher in pitch than when not "fretted." This tone is G on the piano or pitch pipe. Now adjust the second string until it is exactly the same pitch as that produced by the first when "fretted" (fourth fret).

Follow the same procedure for securing the tuning pegs after adjusting the second, third and fourth strings as described for the first string. Tune the third and fourth strings as described for the first string. Tune the third and fourth strings to sound exactly like the second. Now when you strum across the dulcimore, starting with the fourth string and with no strings depressed, you should hear G, G, G, C, in that order. The instrument is now tuned in the key of C. For reasons that will become evident later, the "key of C" tuning is referred to throughout the text. Actually, the dulcimore can be tuned to any pitch; G, A or F seem to be the best, however, if the strings are small in diameter. As a rule of thumb, if the diameters of the strings are equal to the fourth and first strings of a five-stringed banjo, you should tune the dulcimore to G, A or F. If you use one third string and the three first strings of a guitar you can tune the dulcimore to a lower pitch, such as C or D.

The reason for this is fairly obvious. The degree of tension required to prevent the strings from rattling against the frets limits tuning the smaller-diameter strings at the lower musical range. And, while the larger diameter strings will preform well at a lower pitch, it is impractical to tighten them (tune them high) beyond their recommended tension.

The dulcimore is now ready to be played. Grasp the "fretter" (small round stick) between the thumb and fingertips of the left hand, with about 1/2 inch protruding past the thumb and forefinger. This portion of the fretter is placed on the melody string just behind (or to the left) of the third fret. (The frets are numbered from left to right, or from scroll to tailpiece). The fretter should be positioned so that the string is pressed firmly against the fret. When this string is plucked, it should give a nice clear tone. The plucking or strumming is traditionally done with a sharpened goose quill. However, a guitar or mandolin pick is often used, and will give better service, as the quill requires frequent sharpening. Use the thumb or forefinger of the right hand to strum across all four strings until the fretting has been mastered. Make sharp, positive strums, allowing the strings to ring clearly after each strum.

With the fretter behind the third fret, the strings are C, G, G, C. This is the "do" position (diatonic scale). Sliding the fretter down to the position behind the fourth fret produced "re." Going on through the scale, one fret at a time,

3   4   5   6   7   8   9   10 (fret numbers)

do, re, mi, fa, so, la, ti, do,

completes an entire octave. The same relative sequence of tones may be heard on the white keys of a piano if one starts at middle C and progresses up the keyboard, one white key at a time. There are two octaves on a dulcimore. (Note that the tones corresponding to the black keys of a piano are missing.)

Using the method described above, you are now ready to learn to play. After the first few tunes, you will want to play other songs that are familiar. You will start with a "hunt and peck" system, but with practice, you will be able to locate the correct notes automatically.

Now try a simple tune—"My Bonnie Lies Over the Ocean." In the accompanying illustration, fret numbers appear above each syllable. Place the fretter behind the fret represented by these numbers and strum all four strings once for each number. Sing, hum or pronounce each syllable as it is played. Try the tune over and over again until it is completely memorized. As you gain confidence you will find the proper rhythm for the song. The next song, "Skip To Me Lou," is a "play-party" tune, often sung at dances by on-watchers. The strong rhythm is supplied by hand clapping and foot stomping. Sometimes the song is started slowly and with each stanza the tempo increased until the dancers, one by one, drop out.

FIRST SONGS

MY BONNIE LIES OVER THE OCEAN

0　5　4　3　4　3　1　1　0
My bon-nie lies o-ver the o-cean,

0　5　4　3　3　2　3　4
My bon-nie lies o-ver the sea;

0　5　4　3　4　3　1　1　0
My bon-nie lies o-ver the o-cean,

0　1　4　3　2　1　2　3
Oh, bring back my bon-nie to me.

0　3
Bring back,

1　1　4
Oh, bring back,

2　2　2　2　2　1　2　3
Oh, bring back my bon-nie to me.

SKIP TO ME LOU

```
5    5   5  3    5   5   5    7
```
I'll come a-gain, skip to me Lou,

```
4    4   4   2    4   4   4    6
```
I'll come a-gain, skip to me Lou,

```
5    5   5  3    5   5   5    7
```
I'll come a-gain, skip to me Lou,

```
4    6   6   5   4   3   3
```
Skip to me Lou, my dar-ling.

The next tune is a slow ballad. Ballads often had nonsensical lyrics sung with great feeling, or else the lyrics were very meaningful with light, frivolous melodies. "Aunt Rhody's Goose" is of the first type. It should be played slowly and with great feeling.

AUNT RHODY'S GOOSE

```
5   5   4   3   3
```
Go tell Aunt Rho-dy,

```
4   4   6   5   4   3
```
Go tell Aunt Rho - o - dy.

```
7   7   6   5   3
```
Go tell Aunt Rho-dy,

```
3   3   4   3   4   5   3
```
That her old gray goose is dead.

```
3   5   5   4   3   3
```
The one she was sa-ving,

```
4   4   4   6   5   4   3
```
The one she was sa - a - ving,

```
7   7   7   6   5   3
```
The one she was sa-ving,

```
3   4   3   4   5   3
```
To make a fea-ther bed.

In the foregoing examples the rhythm pattern is determined by the poetry of the lyrics; for instance, in "I'll come again, skip to me Lou," the rhythm pattern is simply — — ᴜ —, — — ᴜ — with the dashes indicating long periods and the breves (u) short intervals. If one pronounces a "dah" for long syllables and a "dit" for the short, it would sound like this: "dah dah dit dah, dah dah dit dah." Rhythmically, this is what we try to make the dulcimore say. Practice strumming this pattern on the dulcimore with the melody string open, concentrating on the rhythm while reciting "dah dah dit dah, dah dah dit dah," or "I'll come again, skip to me Lou," in a monotone. Then alternate between the "dah dit" and the lyrics (verbally) to establish a feel for the rhythm of the poetry divorced from any lyrical sentence structure or verbal meaning. The advantage of this will be evident when tunes with no known lyrics are to be learned.

Once the rhythm pattern is established, tones can be assigned to individual syllables by fretting the melody string in the previously described manner. With each number representing a fret, hence a musical tone, a tablature for both the rhythm and tonal characteristics can be constructed. "Skip to me Lou" would look like this:

$$
\begin{array}{cccccccc}
— & — & ᴜ & — & — & — & ᴜ & — \\
5 & 5 & 5 & 3, & 5 & 5 & 5 & 7
\end{array}
$$

$$
\begin{array}{cccccccc}
— & — & ᴜ & — & — & — & ᴜ & — \\
4 & 4 & 4 & 2, & 4 & 4 & 4 & 6
\end{array}
$$

$$
\begin{array}{cccccccc}
— & — & ᴜ & — & — & — & ᴜ & — \\
5 & 5 & 5 & 3, & 5 & 5 & 5 & 7
\end{array}
$$

$$
\begin{array}{ccccccc}
— & — & ᴜ & — & — & — & — \\
4 & 6 & 6 & 5, & 4 & 3 & 3
\end{array}
$$

(Note the break in the rhythm pattern in the last phrase.)

The foregoing can be intoned with "dahs" for long intervals and "dits" for short, thus:

```
5   5   5   3   5   5   5   7
dah dah dit dah, dah dah dit dah

4   4   4   2   4   4   4   6
dah dah dit dah, dah dah dit dah

5   5   5   3   5   5   5   7
dah dah dit dah, dah dah dit dah

4   6   6   5   4   3   3
dah dah dit dah, dah dah dah
```

Of course, writing music in the latter form is intolerably cumbersome. It simply demonstrates the value of having some form of lyrics or phonetics to establish a rhythm pattern.

This tablature method can be used with any song.

THE LITTLE ROSEWOOD CASKET

```
—  ᴗ  —  ᴗ   —     —     ᴗ   —
5  6  7  7   6     4     3   5
In a lit-tle rose-wood cas-ket,

—   ᴗ   —   ᴗ  —   —
5   6   7   7  6   7     5
Rest-ing on a marble stand;

—     ᴗ   —   ᴗ   —   —   ᴗ   —
5     6   7   10  8   6   5   7
There's a pack-age of old let-ters,

—     ᴗ   —   ᴗ   —    ——    —
3     5   4   5   6    5—4    3
Writ-ten by my true lover's hand.
```

Looking at the rhythm pattern using only the dashes and breves and the phonetic "dah dit":

dah dit dah dit dah dah dit dah

dah dit dah dit dah dah dah

dah dit dah dit dah dah dit dah

dah dit dah dit dah dah dah

It is evident that there are really only two rhythmic phrases: — ∪ — ∪ — — ∪ — and — ∪ — ∪ — — —, which are repeated. This is typical of simple music.

Additional stanzas of this beautiful mountain ballad could be included. No doubt, there are many more, either written originally or supplied at a later date by performers to suit their own purposes. In any event, here are sufficient lyrics to form a beautiful story of death and unrequited love:

The melody with rhythm pattern in tablature form is

—	∪	—	∪	—	—	∪	—
5	6	7	7	6	4	3	5

—	∪	—	∪	—	—	—
5	6	7	7	6	7	5

—	∪	—	∪	—	—	∪	—
5	6	7	10	8	6	5	7

—	∪	—	∪	—	——	—
3	5	4	5	6	5—4	3

and some of the lyrics are

Go and bring those letters to me,

A-nd read them all tonight;

I have often tried but could not,

For the tears would blind my sight.

Bring the letters he has written,

He whose voice I've often heard;

Read them over to me sister,

And I'll cherish every word.

A-nd e'er you shall have finished,

Should I calmly fall asleep;

Fall asleep in death and wake not,

Dearest sister do not weep.

In a little rosewood casket,

Resting on a marble stand;

There's a package of old letters,

Written by my true love's hand.

There are certain symbols that appear in many of the old English ballads that were brought to this country and preserved in the Appalachian Mountains. For example, the marble-topped table referred to as a marble stand was popular in 17th- and 18th-century England. The natural coldness of the polished marble is in some way symbolic of the death to come, and the simple beauty of the little rosewood chest or casket speaks of a beautiful love that was lost.

REVIEW OF MUSIC NOTATION

For the benefit of the casual musician, here is a brief review of musical terminology and notation:

1. Modern musical notation is based on the *staff*, which consists of five parallel horizontal lines and associated spaces. When the range of the music goes beyond

that of the staff, additional (ledger) lines are used. Each line and space is called a *degree.*

2. Clefs are placed on the staff to locate the position of one note from which the position of other notes is determined. The most important clef for the dulcimore player is the G Clef, which locates the first G above middle C; it appears on the second line from the bottom. This is easy to remember as the G Clef since its symbol crosses the G line four times, a number greater than on any other line of the staff. (See Figure 25.)

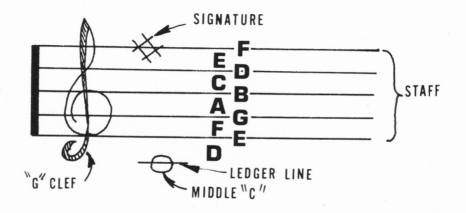

Fig 25 *The G Clef.*

3. A *note* is a character that expresses relative duration by virtue of its shape. When placed on the staff it indicates that the tone assigned to that line or space is to be sounded for a relative period of time determined by the shape of the note.

4. A *sharp* is a symbol that causes the tone or degree of the staff on which it is placed or with which it is associated to be pitched a half step higher than normal.

5. A *flat* is a symbol that causes the tone or degree of the staff on which it is placed to be one half step lower than normal.

6. A *key* is a family of tones bearing a definite and close relationship to one particular tone called the *keynote*.

7. The key is determined by the *signature*, i.e., the sharps and flats or the absence thereof at the beginning of the staff.

8. The *keynote* is the tone of a key to which all others are related. It is normally the note of closing or ending a tune.

Figure 25 shows a staff of five lines and four spaces with one ledger line added below on which middle C is located. The signature of one sharp indicates that the keynote to which all others are related is G, in accordance with the following formula:

1. No sharps or flats in the signature, the key, and consequently the keynote is C major or A minor.

2. One sharp, the keynote is G major or E minor.

3. Two sharps, the keynote is D major or B minor.

4. Three sharps, the keynote is A major or F minor.

5. One flat, the keynote is F major or D minor.

6. Other keys are designated in the same manner, using sharps or flats in the signature. The keys indicated above, however, are sufficient for playing most simple tunes in diatonic modes.

Notice that the signature indicates the major key or its related minor. As one inspects a piece of music, a positive determination of the key, hence the keynote, cannot be made by the signature alone. As pointed out earlier, the keynote is often used to close a tune and the last note to appear on the staff is the keynote. For example, if no sharps or flats appear in the signature and the last note is C, then the tune is in the key of C major; if the last note is A, however, the key is A minor.

EAR, NOTE, TAB AND FINGERBOARD

Now that you have some familiarity with the fingerboard, the tablature and a simple strumming technique, and have received the basic elements of musical notation, you are ready to try techniques for playing the dulcimore from sheet music.

"Down in the Valley" has been chosen to demonstrate tablature construction from sheet music. (See Figure 26.)

First, inspect the music as noted. Looking closely, one sees a quarter note ($\quad$ or $\quad$), a half note ($\quad$ or $\quad$), and a dotted half note ($\quad$ or $\quad$). To each note we assign a symbol that indicates the duration of its tone and mark it directly above the staff. We have chosen a breve ($\cup$) as the symbol for a quarter note (the shortest sounding tone to appear in the song), a bar or dash (—) to indicate a half note, which we have called a long tone, and a double bar (=) to indicate a dotted half, which is the longest tone used. The choice of the symbols is purely arbitrary. Possibly the choice of the double bar (=) for a dotted half is not quite accurate. One might be lead to believe that the dotted half should be held for twice the duration of the half note, which, of course, is not the case. Possibly a better symbol in this case would be a bar dot (÷) to be arithmetically correct. The strongest argument, however, against a rigorous tablature is that this song (among others) is often not rendered in accordance with the music as written. The performer learns the tune and rhythm patterns by ear or by following the notes, and then modifies both to suit his particular needs. Further, it is felt by some that a free-form tune that has been maintained by tradition—that is, verbally—should not be written in such an authoritative, rigorous manner as our system of notes requires. Because a tune appears in one printed document in a given form, it does not necessarily follow that variations of this tune are incorrect. The "correct" notation of the tune would need to include all known variations, if not all *possible* variations. This in some cases could take volumes of print.

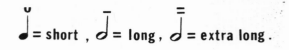

♩ = short , ♩ = long , ♩ = extra long.

"Down in the Valley"

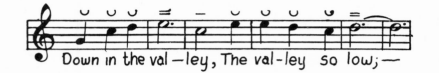

Down in the val—ley, The val—ley so low;—

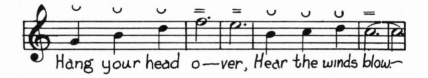

Hang your head o—ver, Hear the winds blow.—

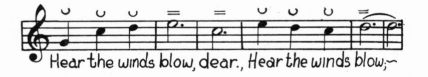

Hear the winds blow, dear., Hear the winds blow;—

Hang your head o—ver, Hear the winds blow.—

Fig 26

After the duration of each of the notes are identified, the tone of each must be established and literally "tied" to the dulcimore fingerboard. Looking at the signature, which always immediately follows the first G Clef, we identify the key as the key of C and our keynote is C above middle C, or the second space from the top of the staff. This note is given a number 3, which assigns it to the third fret, the keynote on the fingerboard with the dulcimore tuned in a standard manner. We could use fret number 10 as the keynote, playing the melody an octave higher. The tablature shown in Figure 27 is in the upper octave.

TABULATURE
"Down in the Valley"

$$\overset{\cup}{7} \quad \overset{\cup}{10} \quad \overset{\cup}{11} \quad \overset{=}{12} \quad \overset{-}{10}, \overset{\cup}{12} \quad \overset{\cup}{12} \quad \overset{\cup}{11} \quad \overset{\cup}{10} \; \overset{=}{11};$$

$$\overset{\cup}{7} \quad \overset{\cup}{9} \quad \overset{\cup}{11} \quad \overset{=}{13} \quad \overset{=}{12}, \overset{\cup}{9} \quad \overset{\cup}{10} \quad \overset{\cup}{11} \quad \overset{=}{10}.$$

$$\overset{\cup}{7} \quad \overset{\cup}{10} \quad \overset{\cup}{11} \quad \overset{=}{12} \quad \overset{=}{10}, \overset{\cup}{12} \quad \overset{\cup}{11} \quad \overset{\cup}{10} \quad \overset{=}{11};$$

$$\overset{\cup}{7} \quad \overset{\cup}{9} \quad \overset{\cup}{11} \quad \overset{=}{13} \quad \overset{=}{12}, \overset{\cup}{9} \quad \overset{\cup}{10} \quad \overset{\cup}{11} \quad \overset{=}{10}.$$

Fig 27

Using 3 as the keynote and assigning it to the second or "C space" on the staff, we can now give fret numbers to all lines and spaces. For instance, the line above C is 4, the next space is 5, the next line is 6, whereas the line below the "C space" is 2, the space below is 1 and the G line is 0, or unfretted. If the tune had called for a tone lower than this, we would be forced to play it in the higher octave. Placing the fret number of each note above the staff, we have a symbol such as $\overline{3}$ or $\overset{\cup}{3}$, which designates not only the tone or position on the fingerboard at which the string is fretted, but also the duration of the tone.

The tablature can be constructed from simple sheet music written in any key so long as the 3rd or the 10th frets are used as the keynote. "Down in the Valley" is written in the key of C and the "C space" is assigned to the third fret. If the dulcimore were tuned to another key, for instance G, the tones produced would automatically transpose the melody to the key of G. The dulcimore (for the most part) can be played in only one key without retuning. This is a definite limitation of the gapped fret arrangement on the dulcimore fingerboard. Using the tablature system, always assigning the keynote to the 3rd or 10th fret, overcomes this limitation to some extent by eliminating the necessity of transposing.

You should perform this tune repeatedly until your playing is quite fluent before proceeding to the next tune. Note the music is in 3/4 time (three beats to a measure) and can be played at a moderate-to-slow tempo.

THE PRETTY MOHEE
(Melody same as On Top of Old Smoky)

As I was out walk-ing
For plea-sure one day,
With sweet rec-ol-lec-tion
I hard-ly can say.

As I sat a-mus-ing
My-self on the grass,
What more should I spy but
A fair In-dian lass.

She sat down be-side me
And tak-ing my hand,
Said you are a strang-er
And in a strange land.

But if you will fol-low
You are wel-come to come,
And dwell with the Mo-hee
In what she calls home.

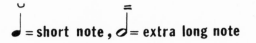

♩ = short note , ♩ = extra long note

THE PRETTY MOHEE

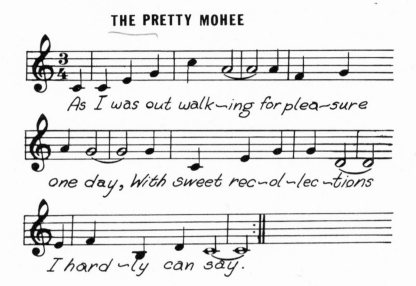

As I was out walk—ing for plea—sure

one day, With sweet rec—ol—lec—tions

I hard—ly can say.

Fig 28

TABLATURE
THE PRETTY MOHEE

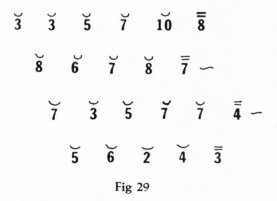

Fig 29

Oh no my sweet dar-ling

That nev-er can be,

For I have a true love

Far o-ver the sea.

And I'll not for-sake her

As I know she won't me,

For she is as true as

The pret-ty Mo-hee.

The last time I saw her

She stood on the sand,

And as I sailed by her

She waved her small hand.

Saying when you get back to

The one that you love,

Re-mem-ber the Mo-hee

In the co-co-nut grove.

And now I am back to

My own na-tive shore,

Friends and re-la-tions

Gather round me once more.

I look all a-round me

But none can I see,

That would ev-er com-pare with

The pret-ty Mo-hee.

This tune probably came to America as "The Sailor and the Lass" via the British shipping lanes. It is a good example of the ability of a tune to live even though the title and lyrics change from generation to generation. The same tune appeared at a later date as "On Top of Old Smoky" with the lyrics

On top of old smok-y
All cov-ered with snow,
I lost my true lov-er
Came court-in' too slow.

"The Little (or Pretty) Mohee" lyrics were introduced during the latter part of the 19th century or the early part of the 20th, and might very well have inspired the "writing" of a rather lengthy series of songs with "Indian Girl" titles—"Silverbells," "Sweet Snowdeer Mine," and "Redwing," to name but a few.

ON MODES AND MINORS AND FLATTED 7TH'S

The fret arrangement on the dulcimore may be likened to the white keys on the piano keyboard. If one starts at middle C on the piano keyboard and moves upward from one white key to the next for a full octave, he will have played a major diatonic scale (do, re, mi, fa, so la, ti, do), in the key of "C." If one starts at the third fret on the dulcimore and moves from one fret to the next (down the frets or to the right), he will have played a major diatonic scale when he reaches the 10th fret. On the piano, black keys are used to supply intermediate notes to make up a chromatic scale. Notice on the piano that there is a black key (C#) following C, a black key (D#) following D, but no black key immediately following E. The next higher key that can be played is F. The same occurs following the next-to-last key in the octave (B to C). Now notice in the dulcimore fret arrangement, there is a relatively wide space between the 3rd and 4th frets and the 4th and 5th, but the space between the 5th and 6th frets is relatively small. In the wider spaces "black key"—equivalent frets are missing!

Thus, the distinguishing feature of the major scale is a full step between the 1st and 2nd and between the 2nd and 3rd tones of the ascending scale (major third). The chromatic or half-step scale is relatively new in the history of music, whereas the "gapped scale" as appears on the dulcimore dates back to ancient times. An arrangement of gapped scales into musical modes originated in Ancient Greece and these scales are followed historically by the medieval or Gregorian and the modern major and minor modes.

The seven Greek modes in which the octave consists of two disjunct tetrachords were reckoned. The four principal ones are the Dorian, Phrygian, Lydian, and Mixolydian. Traditionally these modes were characterized as the Dorian, bold and grave; the Phrygian, brisk and spirited; the Lydian, as soft and sweet, etc.

The medieval or Gregorian modes, which are still used in the Catholic Church, were developed as adaptations of the Ancient Greek modes and bear the same names but differ somewhat in their tonal arrangement. They are made up of a pentachord and a tetrachord in an ascending fashion, with the highest note of one being the lowest note of another. The most interesting of these are the authentic modes. Using a dash (—) for full-step relationship and a breve (∪) for half steps, the medieval modes of interest are as follows:

1. Ionian   C—D—E ∪F —G—A—B ∪C.
2. Dorian   D—E ∪F —G—A—B ∪C—D.
3. Phrygian   E ∪F —G—A—B ∪C—D—E.
4. Lydian   F —G—A—B ∪C—D—E ∪F.
5. Mixolydian G—A—B ∪C—D—E ∪F —G.
6. Aeolian   A—B ∪C—D—E ∪F —G—A.
7. Locrian   B ∪C—D—E ∪F —G—A—B.

One can readily see that the steps and half steps remain fixed in all the modes, with half steps appearing between E and F, and B and C. Referring back to the piano keyboard, starting with C and "walking" the white keys, you will play the Ionian mode; starting with G, the Mixolydian, and with A the Aeolian mode—the three modes of greatest interest to us. The Ionian mode is recognized as the standard modern major mode. The Mixolydian mode is essentially a major scale, with one difference, however; there is no half step between the last two tones. Sometimes this mode is referred to as the flatted 7th mode, or a mode without a "leading tone."

As with the white keys on the piano, "walking" the frets on the melody string, starting at the third, you will play the Ionian mode; starting with the string open, the Mixolydian mode; and starting on the first fret, the Aeolian mode. Thus:

Ionian   3—4—5∪6—7—8—9∪10.

Mixolydian   0—1—2∪3—4—5∪6—7.

Aeolian   1—2∪3—4—5∪6—7—8.

Notice that the Aeolian does not satisfy the requirements for a major scale or mode—two whole steps between the first and third tones. Indeed, this mode is said to have a minor third, thereby qualifying as a *minor* mode. It should not, however, be confused with the modern melodic or the modern harmonic scales, which were developed to eliminate the awkward flatted-7th character of the mode. The modern minor modes cannot be played on a dulcimore without adding frets, in which case one might as well play the guitar, which is more versatile and practical for playing in these modes because of its chromatic scale.

THE MIXOLYDIAN MODE

A vast amount of our simpler music is written in the standard diatonic major mode, which can be referred to as the Ionian mode, if you will; often, however, a tone appears in a song that deviates from the normal major modal sequence of tones. This tone might be an "accidental" or an embellishment or a momentary change of key. In any event, the character of the tune is altered as the "off tones" appear, unexpectedly producing delightful effects.

Whether the tunes were written with full realization of the chromatic scale or whether the composer of the song was "thinking in the Mixolydian mode" or some other medieval mode, is open to debate. It can be assumed that composers were influenced by the medieval modes through exposure to ecclesiastical chants and hymns. In many cases, however, it is believed that such deviations as the flatted 7th (full step between the last two tones of the mode) were used without recognizing the significance of these deviations to the medieval modes. Their appeal to the modern ear seems to be their surprising departure from an anticipated norm. The flatted 7th or the insertion of an extra half step between the 6th and 8th tones in the major scale appears in many of the old mountain tunes as well as some of the "Blues" tunes of the early 1900's. "The Deep Elm Blues" and "John Henry" are examples. To what extent tunes of this type are adaptations of earlier tunes is another area for investigation.

To tune the dulcimore to the Mixolydian mode, that is, so the drones are in harmony with the melody string when the keynote is at "O" or open string, tighten the string. The keynote tone can then be obtained by depressing either the second or third string at the third fret. Tighten the melody string until it sounds exactly like this tone. The eight notes of the scale are

$$0-1-2\cup3-4-5\cup6-7.$$

A classic example of a mountain tune, apparently written in the Mixolydian mode, is "Old Joe Clark." (Figure 30.) This tune was no doubt imported from the British Isles, probably Ireland. In its original form it was in the nature of a "singing song," not being a ballad in the true sense of the word. The fragmented verses, which could be considered original, expound on the dubious feats of a not too popular individual named Joe Clark, Joe Clog, Joe Clerk, or some similar name that could reasonably have been corrupted to "Old Joe Clark." Whether Betty Brown was

OLD JOE CLARK

Fig 30

mentioned originally or became involved with Old Joe after his relocation to the Colonies is also open to question. Verses such as:

> Old Joe Clark's a mighty man,
> And I know what to please him;
> A bottle of wine to make him shine
> And Betty Brown to squeeze him.

(Or "A bottle of ink to make him stink") and:

> He used to live on a mountain top,
> Now he lives in town;
> He's livin' in a Big Hotel
> Courtin' Betty Brown.

certainly show a preoccupation with a relationship between our hero and fair Betty Brown. Other verses have more the flavor of the American Frontier:

> I went down to Old Joe's house,
> Found Old Joe in bed;
> Stuck my finger in Old Joe's eye,
> And killed old Joe down dead.

As a rule these are more crude and nonsensical, akin to:

> How many biscuits can you eat?
> Forty-nine and a chunk of meat.

These verses were obviously invented by lesser endowed poets, perhaps to ridicule some local individual for some deed or lack of accomplishment. Another verse:

> I went down to Old Joe's house,
> Meant to do no harm;
> He pulled out his forty-four,
> And shot me in the arm.

with its reference to a .44 caliber weapon is obviously of relatively recent origin, or at least modification. This line could have read: "He pulled out his old flintlock, or blunderbuss, or horse pistol," or any other type of weapon.

You should now formulate a tablature from the standard notation similar to the one in Figure 31, but in the next higher octave. That is, set the key note on the seventh fret instead of in zero or open position. You can produce delightful variations by leaping from one octave to the other at the beginning of alternate verses or choruses.

THE AEOLIAN MODE

The Aeolian mode is often referred to as the original, normal, primitive or natural minor mode. Its name is derived from Aeolus the God of the Winds, or, more likely, a Grecian tribe named for the God Aeolus. In any event, the Aeolian mode is associated with the wind and plaintive tones produced by the winds blowing through the trees. It is good that the early musicians chose to call this mode "Aeolian." The Aeolian harp or lyre is a many-stringed instrument with a rectangular sound box. The instrument is purportedly played by Aeolus, when hung in an open window.

If one starts with an A key on the piano keyboard and walks the white keys to the next higher A, he will have played the Aeolian scale in the key of A minor. Similarly, if one starts with the first fret on the melody string of a dulcimore and proceeds up the scale, strumming the string at each fret, to the eighth, he will have played a scale in the Aeolian mode in the key in which the dulcimore is tuned. More correctly stated, it will be the related minor key to the major key in which the dulcimore is tuned.

As the drone strings are strummed in playing this scale, it will be noted that they are obviously dissonant with regard to the keynote. This is to be expected as

TABLATURE - 'OLD JOE CLARK'

```
 ‾   ‾   ‾   ‾   ˘   ˘   ‾   ‾   ⹀
 4   4   4   6   5   5   4   3   2

     ‾   ‾   ‾   ‾   ‾   ⹀
     4   4   5   6   5   4

         ‾   ‾   ‾   ‾   ‾   ‾   ⹀
         4   4   5   6   5   4   3   2

             ‾   ‾   ‾   ‾   ⹀
             0   2   1   0   0

                 ‾   ‾   ⹀   ‾   ‾   ⹀
                 0   0   0   4   3   2

                     ‾   ‾   ‾   ‾   ⹀
                     0   0   3   2   1

                         ‾   ‾   ⹀   ‾   ‾   ⹀
                         0   0   0   4   3   2

                             ‾   ‾   ‾   ‾   ⹀
                             0   3   2   1   0
```

Fig 31

the drones were originally tuned to harmonize with the third-fret keynote; as the keynote has been moved to the first fret position, the drones or the melody string must be retuned. It is best and simplest to tune the melody string to match the drone strings.

Do this by sounding the third-fret keynote on the second or third string and adjusting the melody string to sound in unison when depressed at the first fret. To repeat: depress the third string at the third fret; this will give you the tone of the keynote. Then tighten the melody string so that the same tone is heard when the melody string is depressed at the first fret. At this position (the "do" or keynote position) the result of strumming all the strings should sound exactly as the melody string depressed at the third fret in the original (standard) tuning.

When the scale is played again (starting at the first fret) the drones will seem to be in perfect harmony, contrary to what might be expected. We have switched from a major mode to a minor mode and some adjustment of the drone would ordinarily seem necessary. The reason for the consonance is, of course, the absence of a "third" tone, either minor or major, in the chordal structure of the drone harmony. There are the fifth and eighth, with the third present perhaps only in the mind of the listener. Although there is no third string to make up a complete triad (i.e., C E G), the sum of the frequency of vibration of the eighth (C) and the fifth (G), is equal to the frequency of the third (E) in the next higher octave. In the *just scale* this relationship is exact, but in the *tempered scales* there are a few cycles of

Example:

Tone	Frequency of Vibration Cycles per Second
C_4	-
G_4	256
E_5	384
	640

difference, which would not be noticed except by the most discriminating listener.

C_4, E_5, and G_4 form a loose triad. Possibly this is the reason that musicians for many centuries used only the fifth and eighth for harmony. It was not until much later that the third was considered usable and, when it was added, it served only to reinforce that which was already there (one octave removed, of course). I believe that a fine dulcimore is one that reinforces the sum of the frequencies of vibration of the lowest and the highest of the drone strings to the extent that a complete triad is heard, however faintly.

It should be pointed out that again the Aeolian mode is a primitive or basic minor not to be confused with the modern minor scales, of which two exist (melodic and harmonic), neither of which can be played on the dulcimore gapped-fret arrangement.

The Aeolian mode or original minor scale fulfilled the needs of early music adequately. As has been pointed out, it was one of the ancient scales used in the Church before harmony, as we know it today, was developed. With the introduction of part-singing, the need for a leading tone, half step preceding the key tone as in a major scale, became so evident that one was introduced to avoid an otherwise awkward closing. Later, instead of using the "sharpened" or "raised" seventh at the close of a melody only, it was used throughout the music wherever the seventh appeared. Thus the pattern of our modern harmonic minor scale was established.

To play this scale on a dulcimore, one would need to modify the fingerboard by adding a fret between the seventh and eighth frets. Further modification of the fingerboard, such as adding an extra fret between the sixth and seventh frets, would add a leading tone to the Mixolydian mode, thereby converting it to the Ionian or standard major mode. Additional frets throughout the fingerboard would add "black key" tones to the scale structure until all possible tones of the *chromatic* scale were available.

In this "forced evolution" of the dulcimore we would have a fingerboard not unlike that on a guitar. This might appear to be a solution to many of the limitations of the dulcimore. However, each musical instrument has its own set of limitations and efforts to modify it beyond basic improvement of structure and materials often result in changes to the very characteristics that define the instrument.

Many of the old melodies, particularly those of the hill-country songs that can be traced back through history for centuries, were written in the Aeolian mode. In later years the old songs apparently influenced composers to deviate from the more sophisticated modern minor scales to produce pure, simple melodies in the Aeolian mode. Here again it cannot be determined whether the composers recognized in each instance the modal structure of the tunes, or whether they worked from modern minor scales or chromatic scales literally forcing the patterns to produce the desired results. It can be assumed that both might be the case, depending on the composer being considered. "The Wayfaring Stranger" (Figure 32) is one of the old songs written in the Aeolian mode. This song was introduced to the American radio listening public by Burl Ives, who used it as his theme song for many years.

The keynote is assigned to the first fret on the fingerboard. This should correspond to the last note in the music. It is middle C, or one line below the staff. John Putnam would write the fret number designation at the beginning of that line on the staff. Then he would number the lines and spaces up from this line, thereby assigning fret numbers to all notes falling on the different lines. Beginning students can use this technique for reference while constructing a tablature. It is a good practice if one plans to play by note directly without the use of the tablature eventually. I prefer, however, the "over-the-note" notation (after the fashion of Jean Ritchie), with additional symbols to indicate duration.

Work diligently on this tune, observing all rests and note-duration symbols explicitly. Use the thumbstrum method or *stroke* the strings with the index finger,

Wayfaring Stranger

I am a poor way-faring stran-ger, a-trav'ling

through this world of woe, yet there's no sick-ness, toil or

dan-ger in that bright world to which I go.

CHORUS

I'm go-ing home — to see my father, I'm go-ing there

no more to roam; I'm on-ly go——ing o-ver

Jor—dan, I'm on-ly go——ing o-ver home.

Fig 32

rapidly for the shorter notes and slowly for the longer ones. The tune should be played slowly and with great feeling.

Other tunes to try in the Aeolian mode are "We Three Kings of Orient Are", "St. James Infirmary Blues," and "God Rest Ye Merry Gentlemen."

ACCOMPANYING WITH A DULCIMORE

The dulcimore may be used to accompany the singing voice or another instrument. One effective technique is to play an alto or tenor part on the melody string and allow the drones to provide the harmony on the keynote as if one were playing the melody. The result is very beautiful, especially if the lead instrument is another dulcimore. This technique is often used with the double dulcimore such as the "Harmonium" or the courting dulcimore. Sometimes, too, with these double instruments, a bass part can be very effective if the accompaniment strings are tuned one octave lower than the lead strings. Indeed, if one wishes, the fretting stick may be laid aside and the fingers used to stop the strings at an appropriate fret to provide two or three-part harmony.

The simplest method of accompanying a singer or another instrument is to form basic chords. (A chord is a group of tones, three or more, sounded together and bearing a harmonic relationship to each other. The simplest chord is a "triad," *tri* meaning three.) Use the fingers instead of the fretter; the position of the fingers relative to the various frets depends, of course, on the tuning arrangement of the strings.

There are several interesting ways to vary the tuning. One very effective method is to deviate from the normal "fifth" tuning arrangement, and tune the dulcimore so that a complete triad or chord is played when the open strings are strummed. As an example, the first string is tuned to middle C, the second string to the third above that, or E, and the third string to the fifth above the C, or G. If a four-stringed dulcimore is used the fourth or melody string can be tuned in unison with the third. Now we have a triad C E G, with the G repeated. By simply barring the strings with the index finger we can stop all strings at any fret we wish. With strings open, the chord is a triad in C, stopped at the first fret it is a triad in D, at the second fret in E, third in F, and stopping at the fourth fret gives a triad rooted in G. Continuing down the fingerboard gives triads rooted in progressively higher keys in accordance with the diatonic scale.

As an alternative tuning for a four-stringed dulcimore, the first three strings may be tuned to C E G. The fourth or melody string may then be tuned one octave above the first string, giving C E G C, which forms a rich four-part chord by doubling the root. When the strings are barred at the third fret, for instance, the chord becomes F A C F, a chord rooted in F, and at the fourth fret, G B D G, a chord rooted in G. Chords of C, D, E, F, G, A and B♭ may be formed by simply barring the strings at the appropriate frets. All these are classed as major chords; the formation of minor chords is more complex and the tuning for "bar chords" should not be used.

In forming the harmony for singing or other "lead" music, it is usually sufficient to use the *primary chords* of the key in which the melody is rendered. The primary chords are composed of the triad of the key tone or "tonic" chord, a second triad which is rooted four tones higher (counting the tonic as one), often called the "subdominant," and a third chord which is five tones higher than the key tone, called the "dominant." These chords are usually numbered I, IV, V, Roman numerals being used to avoid confusion with firsts, thirds, fifths, etc., which are designations on individual tones.

Table I shows the chords in the various keys available with this tuning arrange-

TABLE I
CHORDS OBTAINABLE IN VARIOUS AVAILABLE KEYS

KEY=C

FRET NO.	CHORDS	TONES
0	I	C E G C'
3	IV	F A C F'
4	V	G B D G'

KEY=D

1	I	D F# A D
4	IV	G B D G'
5	V	A C# E A'

KEY=A

5	I	A C# E A'
1	IV	D F# A D'
2	V	E G# B E

KEY=G

4	I	G B D G'
0 or 7	IV	C E G C'
1	V	D E# A D'

KEY= F

3	I	F A C F'
6	IV	Bb D F Bb
7	V	C E G C'

ment, obtained by simply barring the fret as indicated under the column marked "frets." The Roman numeral under the column marked "chords" indicates the chord's position within the key. The tones produced by the strings when they are strummed toward the player are also shown. Under "key of C" it is obvious that the instrument is tuned to the key of C, since the tonic chord (I) is sounded when the strings are not stopped (fret No. 0). The tones formed are C E G (when strummed toward the player), and a tone one octave above the first (C'). The subdominant chord (IV), F A C F' is sounded when the strings are stopped at the third fret, and the dominant (V) when they are stopped at the fourth fret. The chords are called C, F, and G and are I, IV, and V for the key of C.

Similarly, positioning I at the first fret and stopping fourth and fifth frets for IV and V, respectively, will give D, G and A—the primary chords in the key of D.

Chords can be formed with the dulcimore tuned in the standard mode, that is, G G C for the three-stringed instrument or G G G C for the four-stringed instrument. Forming chords is most easily mastered on a three-stringed instrument in the following manner: Stop the middle string with the ring finger at the fifth fret. The tone of this string is E above the keynote. The first string is played open, as is the third string. Strumming away from the player the tones are G E' C, or if the strumming is reversed, C E' G, which is a triad on the key of C. Admittedly, the E' is an octave higher than the E falling midway between the C and G, which is formed by the open first and third strings. This, however, is musically acceptable. This chord may be used as "I" in the I, IV, V sequence previously discussed.

As the C chord is the first in a sequence, we know that the second or *subdominant* chord should be F, and the dominant or "V" should be G. The F triad is formed with the tones F A C. Stop the middle string at the sixth fret to sound F. The first string is left open to provide the C; to form the A, drop the thumb to the third string at the eighth fret; the triad IV is formed. For the V triad, or G, the tones G B D are needed. To obtain B the thumb is used to stop the third (melody) string at the ninth fret, while the ring finger provides a G at the seventh fret. As an alternative the G can be sounded with the middle string open. The D is provided with the index finger on the first string at the eighth fret.

As I, IV and V often follow in a normal sequence, they may be practiced in the following manner:

1. With ring finger on the second string, at the fifth fret, strum all three strings for a measured number of beats.

2. *Slide* ring finger down the second string to the next fret (sixth) and drop the thumb to the third string at the eighth fret. Strum all strings as on the previous chord. Try to make the change without losing the beat.

3. *Slide* the ring finger and the thumb down one fret so that the ring finger is on the seventh fret and the thumb on the ninth. Drop the index finger to the first string at the eighth fret and strum as before.

4. Practice this sequence repeatedly until all movements can be made without disturbing the steady beat. A metronome or similar pacing device would be useful at this point. After suitable progress has been made, the order of the chords should be changed from I, IV, V, I, to I, IV, I, V, I, or I, V, I, IV, V, I. Practice various rhythm patterns when you can make chord changes with sufficient dexterity.

With this chording technique, you are limited to playing in the key to which the instrument is tuned. Here again the key of C was used as an example. If the instrument is tuned to any other key, the finger positions are the same.

SOME ADDITIONAL SONGS FOR PRACTICE

Fig's 33 through 36 are four well-known tunes. The first, "Red River Valley," is an old cowboy song, a classic in American folk music. The second is a favorite among students of folk music, known as "Barbara Allen," "Barbry Allen" or "Ellen," according to its many variations. There are at least four variations in the melody, some in the Aeolian mode (minor). No two performers sing the song to the same tune. The arrangement shown here is probably a culmination of many others. There are so many verses to this old ballad that I have lost count. (At one time I knew 97, many of them repetitious and adding nothing to the story.) Others are standard verses from songs of this type and from this period, either borrowed from or lent to other ballads. Even though the lyrics are altered, the story seems to remain the same—Sweet William is dying for the love of one Barbra Allen who is piqued because of some real or imaginary slight and refuses to console him. After his death she is filled with remorse and dies of grief. The theme of the briar growing on her grave and a rose on his is quite common in ballads of this period.

"Amazing Grace" is such a popular song that little need be said about it. This arrangement has both the lead part and the alto. You should learn both parts and practice, alternating from lead to alto, playing the lead through once then singing the lead while you play the alto part. Then play the lead part, etc. Play it slowly in freestyle, one strum of the strings for each note.

The next practice song is known under other names and there are other songs also called "The Riddle Song." However, the name is appropriate in that a riddle is asked and answered in the lyrics. This is another freestyle song. No rhythm not evident in the notation is necessary—just strum the strings once for each note.

RED RIVER VALLEY

From this val ley they say you are go—ing——. We will miss your bright eyes and sweet smile for they say you are tak—ing the sun - shine—— That has brightened our path -way a - while

Fig 33

ADDITIONAL VERSES TO RED RIVER VALLEY

2. Come sit by my side e'er you leave home,
    Do not hasten to bid me adieu,
    But remember the Red River Valley
    And the cowboy who loved you so true.

3. Won't you think of the valley you're leaving?
    Oh how sad and lonely it will be.
    Won't you think of the heart you are breaking,
    And the pain you are causing to me?

BARBARA ALLEN

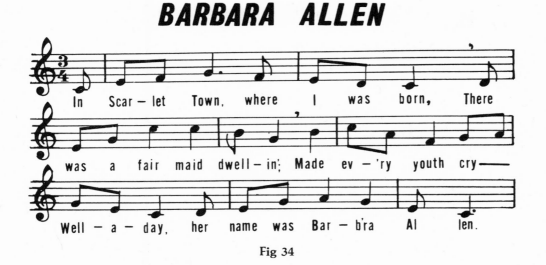

In Scar — let Town, where I was born, There
was a fair maid dwell — in; Made ev — 'ry youth cry——
Well — a — day, her name was Bar — b'ra Al len.

Fig 34

ADDITIONAL LYRICS FOR BARBRA ALLEN

1. It was in the merry month of May
   When all things were a-bloomin'
   Sweet William on his deathbed lay
   For the love of Barbra Allen.

2. He sent his servant to the town,
   To the place where she was dwellin'
   Sweet William's sick and sends for you
   If your name be Barbra Allen.

3. So slowly, slowly she got up,
   And slowly she drew nigh him,
   And all she said when she got there
   Was "Young man, I think you're dyin."

4. Oh yes, I'm sick, so very sick,
   And death is in me dwellin'
   No better, no better will I ever be
   If I can't have Barbra Allen.

5. Oh yes you're sick, so very sick,
   And death is in you dwellin'
   No better no better you'll ever be,
   For you can't have Barbra Allen.

6. In a tavern over in yonder town,
   In the place where you are dwellin'
   You drank the health of the ladies round,
   But slighted Barbra Allen.

7. As she was on her way back home,
   The birds they all were singin',
   And as they sang, they seemed to say,
   Hard hearted Barbra Allen.

8. She turned to the east, she turned to the west,
   She spied his mourners comin'
   Lay down, lay down that corpse of clay
   And let me look upon him.

9. The more she looked the more she mourned
   She fell to the ground a cryin',
   Said take me home, oh take me home
   For I think that I am dyin'.

10. Mother, oh Mother go make my bed,
    Go make it long and narrer,
    Sweet William died for me today,
    And I'll die for him tomarrer.

11. They buried her in the old church yard,
    They buried William nigh her.
    And on his grave grew a big red rose,
    On Barbra's grew a briar.

12. They grew and grew to the old church tower,
    Till they could grow no higher,
    And twined they were in a true lover's knot,
    With the rose growin' 'round the briar.

AMAZING GRACE

Fig 35

The Riddle Song

I gave my love a cher~ry that had no stone.

I gave my love a chick~en that had no bone;

I gave my love a ring that had no— end;

I gave my love a ba—by, with no cry—ing?

Fig 36

ADDITIONAL VERSES TO THE RIDDLE SONG

How can there be a cherry that has no stone;
A cherry when it's blooming it has no stone;

How can there be a chicken that has no bone;
A chicken when it's pipping it has no bone;

How can there be a ring that has no end;
A ring when it's rolling it has no end;

How can there be a baby with no crying?
A baby when it's sleeping, there's no cry-ing.

In this tune the melody does not end on the keynote, but drops to the fifth, seemingly leaving the melody unresolved. On the final verse a performer will often return to the keynote in order to terminate the tune, since the last verse is a series of answers to questions asked in the preceding verses and does indeed resolve the riddle.

BAGPIPE TUNES

"The Green Hills of Tyrol" and "Scotland the Brave" are old Scottish bagpipe tunes which, to my knowledge, have no lyrics. Setting the music in standard notation is quite difficult because of the nature of the chanter pipe which requires that grace notes (notes that are considered an ornament and not a part of the melody, but must be played to progress from one note to the other) be inserted. It is often difficult to distinguish the grace notes from the melody notes. Ideally though, they are of such short duration that the ear barely perceives them. I have set these songs in tablature form. The short notes, indicated by the breves, should be played as eighth notes, and the long, indicated by short lines, as quarter notes except at the end of each part when the notes should be held for a longer period of time.

These songs can be played in the normal or Ionian tuning, but if you would like to produce a more distinct bagpipe sound, tune the middle drones to the keynote, press the melody string at the third fret, and tune the two small drone strings to match this tone. If you play a three-string dulcimore, you tune only the middle string.

SCOTLAND THE BRAVE

U — — U U U U — — U U U U
7 3 3 4 5 3 7 10 10 10 7 5 3

— U U — U U — — U U U U U U
6 8 6 5 7 5 4 7 7 8 7 6 5 4

— U U U U U U — — U U U U
3 3 4 5 3 5 7 10 10 10 7 5 3

— U U U U U U U U U —
6 8 6 5 7 5 3 4 3 4 3 (repeat)

— — — U U U —
7 10 10 10 7 5 3

— — U U U —
10 10 10 7 5 7

— U U — U U — — U U U U U U
6 8 6 5 7 5 4 7 7 8 7 6 5 4

— U U U U U U — — U U U U
3 3 4 5 3 5 7 10 10 10 7 5 3

— U U U U U U U U U —
6 8 6 5 7 5 3 4 3 4 3 (repeat)

Fig 37

THE GREEN HILLS OF TYROL

U U – U U U U – U U U U U U –
3 4 5 5 3 5 6 7 7 8 5 8 7 5 4

U U U U –
4 8 7 5 3

U U – U U U – U U U U U –
3 4 5 5 3 5 6 7 7 8 5 8 7 5 4

U U – –
4 3 5 3 (repeat)

U U – – U U U U – U U U U – U
5 7 10 10 9 8 8 7 7 7 8 7 6 6 6

U U U –
7 6 5 5

U U – – U U U U – U U – U U
5 7 10 10 9 8 8 7 7 7 8 7 7 6

U U – –
5 6 7 7 (repeat)

Fig 38

OTHERS

WILDWOOD FLOWER

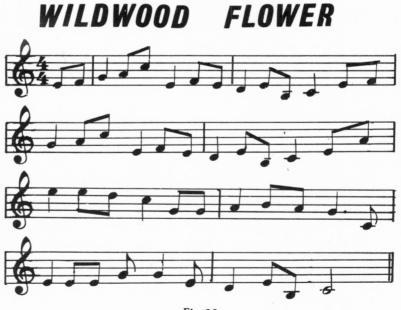

Fig 39

WILDWOOD FLOWER

I will dance, I will sing,
and my laugh will be gay,
I will charm every heart
in the crowd I will sway,
but when I awoke, all my idols were clay,
all passions for life had all passed away.

Oh I'll twine with my mangles of waving black hair,
With the roses so red and the lilies so fair,
and the myrtle so bright from the emerald dew,
the pale and the leider with eyes look like blue.

He taught me to love him and promised to love,
and to cherish me over all others above,
my heart now is yearning, no misery can tell,
he left me no warning, no word of farewell.

He promised to love me and called me his flower,
a blossom to cheer him in life's golden hour,
but now he is gone and left me forlorn
with the wild flowers to weep and the wild birds to mourn.

I will dance, I will sing,
and my life will be gay,
I will charm every heart
in this crowd I will sway,
but I'll live yet to see him regret that dark hour
that he's gone and neglected this wild woodland flower.

Fig 40

THE FOUR MARYS

U — U U U U — —
3 5 4 3 5 7 8 7

U — U U U U =
3 5 5 7 6 5 4

U U — — U U U — — U U
7 7 10 10 9 9 8 7 5 3 3

U — U U U U U =
4 5 6 5 4 5 4 3

Fig 41

Last night there were four Marys,
Tonight there'll be but three;
There was Mary Seaton and Mary Beaton,
and Mary Carmichle and me.

Oh, Often have I dressed my queen,
and put on her braw silk gown;
But all the thanks I've tonight,
is to be hanged in Edinborough town.

Oh, little did my mother know,
the day she cradled me;
The land I was to travel in,
the death I was to dee.

Oh, happy, happy is the maid
that's born of beauty free;
Oh it was my rosy, dimpled cheeks
that's been the devil to me.

They'll tie a kerchief around my eyes
that I may not see to dee;
And they'll never tell my father or mother,
But that I'm across the sea.

Fig 42

Pattern Guide Sheet
Master Assembly
Jig Pattern

This pattern is to be used in lieu of the handmade pattern described under "The pattern."

The following instructions are numbered to correspond to numbered parts on the Master Assembly Jig Pattern:

1. *Center section of sides.* Trace this curve on 2-by-6-inch stock and cut to form dies in accordance with section titled "side-forming dies" and Fig. 4.

2. Same as 1. Follow section on forming the sides and refer to figures therein.

3. Drive four-penny finishing nails into the jig at these points. See section on "Master assembly jig" and Fig. 5. Follow the section on "Jigging the Sides."

4 & 5. See Section on "Bracing," and the accompanying sketches. Cut cross braces to fit the pattern.

6 & 7. See section on "bracing" and fig. 8a.

8. Cut this glue block of 2-inch stock to fit the curvature of the side pieces. Drive additional nails into the assembly jig as needed.

9. Same as 8.

10. Tuning head in place.

11. *Tuning head pattern.* Study section on "Tuning head." Trace this pattern on these 1/2-inch pieces to form sandwich. Cut out the center section to conform to dashed line. Cut the two outside sections to follow spiral. Cut mortises at right angles, as in the pattern, top view. Drill peg holes 1/4 inch then shape with tapered reamer to 3/8 inch as shown.

12. *Trailing Heart Sound Hole.* Complete the soundboard as described in section titled "The Soundboard." Place the trailing heart sound hole approximately in the position shown in Fig. 17. The exact location is not important; however, it should be located near the positions shown. Round sound holes approximately 1 inch in diameter should also be provided as shown in Fig. 1a.

13. *The fingerboard* pattern gives you the positioning of the nut, frets and bridge on the sound bar and the "strum hollow" cross section. The sections describing the sound bar and its construction should be your guide. After sound bar is assembled, place this pattern on the top and trace fret, nut and bridge positions carefully. The round hole near the left-hand end of the pattern is optional.

14. *Tailpiece.* See section on "Completing the sides." Although the exact shape of this piece is optional, the critical dimensions should be observed.

15. *Tuning pegs.* See section titled "Tuning Pegs." Violin, or preferably viola pegs, may be substituted for these handmade pegs. Note that the pegs are tapered from 3/8 inch to 1/4 inch to match tapered holes in tuning head. If viola pegs are used, the holes must be made to fit those pegs.

16. *Fingerboard endpiece.* This piece can be made from scraps. It is glued to the left-hand end of the sound bar to close the end. Its use, however, is optional.

Afterword

From the onset I knew that the writing of this book would be a monumental task. The collection and organization of information that had been 'common everyday facts' to me into a readable publication was not easily done, nor at the onset was I easily convinced of the need for it. For the last 25 years I have shown my dulcimores at arts and crafts exhibits such as the 'American Folk Life Festival' at the Smithsonian Institution, and I have demonstrated and lectured at schools, universities, and museums throughout the country. At each gathering I am amazed at the thirst for knowledge that exists in the public. . . . Where did the dulcimore come from? Who invented it? What were the people like? How do you make it? How long does it take? How is it played? Where? Why? What? How much? During the course of the years I became convinced that a book was needed, indeed, and I eagerly awaited the writing of an 'answerbook' by one of my peers. Alas, so I've learned, they, too, have problems, their own sets of questions and answers, and if a book were to be written which would tell *my* story, it would have to be written by *me*.

The realization that a book was needed and that it needed to be written by me was not, however, sufficient motivation. This stage in book writing has been reached by many. Here lies the "many good books that were never written." The missing ingredient needed to move my book from this stage to the next or completed stage was faith. It was not so much faith in myself or belief in my ability to do this (we are all inclined to feel that we *can* do it if we really "set to it"), but the belief of others that I *would* do it that gave me the confidence and fortitude to neglect easier tasks and press on with this writing. It is to these people and their faith that I dedicate this book, this footprint, this part of my life set down for all to see.

I must first mention the role played by my wife *Irene* and daughter *Patricia*. They provided me with the real motivation; their love and understanding. Then there is: *Roy Acuff* who befriended me and by publicly admiring my craft inspired me to do even better. *George Herman* whose dedication to folklore and folk crafts has been a veritable stimulant to me, *Mary L. McMurtrie* who minded my p's & q's throughout this writing and *Harry Wilson* who provided the handsome sketches and drawings throughout the book, the many members of *The Mountain Dulcimore Society* who have eagerly awaited this publication, and last, my good friend, *Ray Smith* who provided the art work for the book jacket and who expressed in verse what I cannot, even in prose:

ON DULCIMORES AND FRIENDS
(by *Ray Smith*)

The hills of Appalachia emit a pleasant haunting ring
Of mountain music played from just a single string.
One string—then two or three, progressing then to four.
From man's love for native music evolved the Dulcimore.

The craftsmanship is crude, there's rust upon the strings,
But the sound that warms the heart makes these just minor things.
This crude mountain instrument of a mountain craftsman's hands,
Makes footprints on the hearts of men as well as on life's sands.

It builds and welds true friendships as if through well laid plans,
Leaving footprints on the hearts of men from similar, yet different lands.
A friendship can't be purchased, it's one of life's treasured things,
And to think it all transpired from just four rusty strings.

I could have looked and searched forever for such a treasured friend,
I could have traveled every river, and searched out every bend,
But true friends aren't simply found, they're made by simple things,
Like the mountain craftsman's Dulcimore with the four rusty strings.

Though your life sometimes gets rusty, as did these mountain strings,
Clean off the rust and use it, you'll see the friends and hope it brings.
Let it leave some footprints on the hearts of worthy men,
And when you cross that river may the footprints never end.

Chet Hines